Summoning Forth Wiccan Gods and Goddesses

SUMMONING FORTH
WICCAN GODS
AND GODDESSES

The Magick of Invocation and Evocation

꙳S꙳

Lady Maeve Rhea, HPS
MotherChant Coven

A CITADEL PRESS BOOK
Published by Carol Publishing Group

A Citadel Press Book
Published by Carol Publishing Group
Citadel Press is a registered trademark of Carol Communications, Inc.

Editorial, sales and distribution, rights and permissions inquiries should be
addressed to Carol Publishing Group, 120 Enterprise Avenue, Secaucus, N.J.
07094.

In Canada: Canadian Manda Group, One Atlantic Avenue, Suite 105,
Toronto, Ontario M6K 3E7

Carol Publishing Group books may be purchased in bulk at special discounts
for sales promotion, fund-raising, or educational purposes. Special editions
can be created to specifications. For details, contact Special Sales
Department, Carol Publishing Group, 120 Enterprise Avenue, Secaucus, N.J.
07094.

Manufactured in the United States of America

10 9 8 7 6 5 4 3 2 1

Library of Congress Cataloging-in-Publication Data

Rhea, Maeve.
    Summoning forth Wiccan gods and goddesses : the magick of
invocation and evocation / by Maeve Rhea (Barbara E. Vordebrueggen).
        p. cm.
    "A Citadel Press book."
    Includes bibliographical references.
    ISBN 0–8065–2039–6 (pbk.)
    1. Magic. 2. Witchcraft. 3. Gods—Miscellanea. 4. Invocation—
Miscellanea. 5. Evocation—Miscellanea. I. Title.
BF1623.G63R48   1998
133.4'3—dc21   98–34834
                                                        CIP

CONTENTS

PART III: EVOCATION

PART IV: PITFALLS AND POSSIBILITIES

PREFACE

Dear Reader,

I open my book with a few words to you. By the time you have finished this book, you will know a lot about me, and if you practice the techniques and arts that I am going to teach you, I will come to know a lot about you. When you have learned what this book has to teach you, you will understand that statement.

I already know this: you are intelligent and curious. It is likely that you are open-minded and driven by a need to expand your internal boundaries. I know that you are committed, and I hope, patient, but if you do not consider patience to be one of your strong suits, do not despair. I am an incredibly impatient person and I was able to master these techniques.

What I am going to teach you in this book—or more appropriately stated, show you how to learn for yourself—are techniques that will allow you to take back an ancient birthright.

You were born with an ability that our pan-world culture and the dominant religions of our world have stolen from you.

You were born with the ability to have a personal one-on-one direct experience of the Divine.

You were born with the ability to communicate directly and share those communications with others.

All that and more was taken away from you. In effect, you have been spiritually crippled. This book and the information it contains will help you begin the process of healing yourself and the biosphere around you.

What I am going to teach you is not a supernatural power. There are no supernatural powers; there are only energies that our primitive sciences cannot yet detect or measure. But simply because our scientists and engineers haven't yet figured out ways to recognize, measure, and manipulate these energies, there is no reason why you shouldn't, except in cases where doing so would be injurious to yourself or others.

We must always keep in mind that today's magicks are tomorrow's sciences. A thousand years ago, anyone who had understood the energy of electricity would have been burned as a heretic or sorcerer. In Elizabethan times, an English merchant *was* burned for practicing Witchcraft because he knew how to multiply numbers. About 120 years ago, an Anglican bishop made the statement that everything that could be discovered had been, and that all future advances would merely be the refining of those discoveries. I wonder what that bishop would say if he could see me typing on my computer and discussing ideas over the Internet with friends on the other side of the world.

Given this kind of cultural history, it is not surprising that scientists and members of the dominant religions believe that the energies that I am going to show you how to use are either nonexistent or evil. However, thousands of years ago, people did know how to manipulate those energies; they did have the sciences, or perhaps a more apt word would be *arts*, that enabled them to do things that today are considered impossible. These arts were once known and practiced widely, and then, starting about 2,500 years ago, they were for many reasons suppressed and persecuted, and finally mostly forgotten.

One of the most important and powerful of these arts is invocation of Divinity. The evocation of the gods is another. And those two arts are what I am going to teach you. I am going to show you how to have, safely and sanely, one of the most ecstatic and powerful experiences in the universe.

Read this book carefully and thoroughly before trying any of these exercises. Then go back to the beginning and do the exercises and meditations. Finally, when that wise part of yourself says that you are ready, you will find yourself stepping naturally and gracefully into the states of invocation and evocation.

In this book I will use terms that may be unfamiliar to you. They are probably terms or words that I have made up to suit my need for communication. I shall try to define them clearly and supply you with a graphic metaphor, but if you are stumped, simply ask your wise self what he or she thinks I mean. I am almost certain that you will get a correct reply.

Now, about believing—that big, underlined, italicized thing in our lives. I would caution you to believe in little, except gravity. If you find yourself in a situation in which someone or something demands that you—without question—believe what they are saying, get out of there!

Always question authority. Never accept without question that someone knows better than you, that they are wiser or more enlightened. Obey the laws of your state and country—it usually makes things safer and more comfortable—but if something bothers you, question it. There was once a law that said that women couldn't vote. A lot of brave people questioned it, and that law was set aside.

There is a "belief" that no one (or perhaps only very "holy" people) can have direct apprehension of Divinity. That belief is a lie. It is a conscious and deliberate lie, invented long ago by authoritarian religious groups that wished to weaken and control others. It is time for that belief also to be set aside.

Don't believe anything I write in this book simply because I write it. Try the techniques, practice them, do the exercises, and find out for yourself. The work that I will put before you will be painful at times—healing one's psychic body can be as painful as healing one's physical body. But there are no shortcuts, no quick answers, no "miracle drugs" that will do this work for you. It may take weeks, months, or even years before you become proficient, but you *can* do it. And when you have done so, you, your internal universe, and the world around you will never be the same again.

PART I

Preparation

1

Introducing the Concepts of Invocation and Evocation

The light is intense but in no way causes distress. The sounds are clear, scintillating, and harmonious. The sensation of complete acceptance washes through the woman as she floats in a state of bliss. Here, in this place of no particular being, she finds complete love, complete oneness. As she floats, she perceives visual objects surrounding her: stars, planets, and beings from other dimensions, other places, other times. She hears exquisite music that at once comes from inside of her and all around her. She is home.

Then the light takes form—a female form, for that is what the woman is most comfortable with at this moment. The form is at once of youthful beauty and ancient wisdom. The form touches the woman and the two dance in a swirl of stars. The form speaks within the woman's being: "Remember, I have always loved you. There is nothing that you can do that will make me cease to love you, or to change my love of you one whit. I love you because you are not perfect. I love you because of your faults. If you were perfect, you would be stagnant, dead. Because you are not perfect, you are alive, growing, learning, able to be what and who I need—want—you to be."

Then the Form blends back into the light, the woman floats for a moment more—an eternity—and then slowly sinks back into the physical form that awaits her.

The woman finds that she is lying on the floor. Once more in her own body, her own living room, in a house in suburban North America, she sits up. She aches slightly, feeling both energized and drained; she feels the power slipping away. Yet she has been changed. Her ability to retain some of the bliss, some of the power, has been increased.

As she looks around her, she sees that several of the members of her circle are still in a state of ungrounded energy. Slowly, carefully, she goes to each one and helps them release the excess energy of the ritual. Then, together with them, she releases the evoked energies of the Directional Guardians.

What I have just described to you is one of my personal experiences while in a state of invocation. Invocation is a process by which an individual makes a psychic, that is, emotional and mental, space within themselves. Into this space the person will welcome the energy of one of the facets of Divinity. I call a facet or aspect of Divinity a God-form. (Gods express themselves as both female and male. Since Divinity is genderless in nature but differentiates Itself into female and male only to facilitate our perception of It, I do not usually use the term Goddess-form; God-form suffices.)

While in a state of invocation, the person may be completely present, or she may slip into a trance state wherein she may experience mystical union and comprehension with Divinity. She may receive messages or prophecy and travel into other dimensions of reality and time. While in the trance state, she may speak to others, giving them messages that she will not recall when she has returned to her ordinary state of consciousness. She may be able to accomplish things that she would not normally be able to do, such as doing high jumps with arthritic joints, or seeing clearly without lenses when she normally has to wear corrective lenses at all times. She may experience new forms of energy manifestation from objects usually thought to be inert. Rocks, trees, and water may shimmer and pulse with energy. A sense of utter union with the entire universe may accompany these perceptions.

Evocation is a process in which a person or group of people make a psychic space into which they invite God-Forms to manifest themselves as the God-forms choose. Thus, a Wiccan circle, which usually includes the summoning of the Directional Guardians of North, West, South, and East and/or the Elemental Guardians of Earth, Air, Fire, and Water, may find that the southern direction manifests itself as a Fire God-form, such as Agni from Persian mythology, or Lugh from Celtic mythology, or even Apollo from the Hellenic mythos. Indeed, it might manifest itself as a volcano, or even as Pele from the Polynesian myths.

The other directions could also manifest as well-known classical God-forms, or they might take the shapes of animals or nature spirits such as Nymphs, Sylphs, Dryads, Sphinxes.

Elemental and Directional Guardian God-forms are not the only aspects of Divinity that are evoked into a sacred space or circle. Often a specific God-form is desired to increase the power and intent of the ritual. A healing ritual may call for the evocation of Asclepias, or Bridgidh. A protection ritual might call for Auge (Bear), or Isis, or even for Lilith. A ritual of divination might ask Heka to come, accompanied by Her Son, Iacchos. Who or what might be evoked into the sacred space is only limited by the energy and power of the people who have created the space.

Both invocation and evocation are accomplished by the intentions and the power of the persons involved in the ritual. Both magickal acts must be approached with care and preparation. Both are extremely powerful.

While invocation and evocation have much in common, their differences are important. While evocation can be effected by a group or a single practitioner, invocation is a solitary experience. Others may provide an enhanced and sacred space, but the act of invocation belongs to the invoker. A ritual may include both acts, or either one alone, or neither. It all depends on the purpose of the ritual and the intentions of the persons involved.

When considering whether you wish to invoke a god-form, evoke god-forms or elemental beings, or do both, or neither, carefully consider what you intend to accomplish with the ritual. Most rituals do not need an invocation or evocation.

Let me summarize:

Invocation is a process in which a person, acting as a single individual, allows an aspect of Divinity that I call a god-form to enter into her or his body.

Evocation is a process in which a person or group invites an aspect of Divinity, such as an Elemental or Directional guardian, or a specific God-form, into the working space as defined by the ritual.

2

Definitions of Divinity

ॐ

I know you are asking, how can anyone "tell" a God or Goddess to show up in a given place, or time, and in a comprehensible manner? Your question is apt, for one tells the Gods nothing. One invites them, with love and pride, and rests secure with the knowledge that Divinity will enjoy the dance as much as the person doing the invoking.

Let me step back and define exactly what I mean when I use the terms Divinity and God-form.

It is not possible to comprehend Divinity. We have neither the physical nor the mental equipment.

About the best that can be done is acknowledge that Divinity is that which is and which is not. *Ohm Agus Nah-Ohm*: That Which is Some-thing and That Which is No-thing. *No-thing* does not mean "nothing," it means "no particular thingness"—a state of not being any particular way, rather than a state of absolute nonbeing. You can think of No-thingness as the space that allows the Some-things to exist. It is latency, possibility, promise.

But human minds desire very deeply to understand as much about Divinity as possible, so we have created God-forms to suit our needs, environment, and aspirations. Trying to comprehend the "Great White Light" is a waste of human energy. One can learn nothing from staring into it. We need definition and demarcation, to be able to communicate and learn.

Imagine that Divinity is an infinite incomprehensible jewel with an infinite number of facets through which the energy of the Divine is refracted in innumerable ways. In the course of human existence, human beings come into contact with aspects of life that manifest Divinity; its creativity, power, wisdom, caring. Whether or not they are conscious of it, humans are affected by, and affect, this Divine energy. Then they shape the energy according to their needs—hunting, healing, fertility and childbirth, coming of age, growing old, and finally death—all the things that are basic to human life.

In response to their environment, humans also shape the energy flowing through the facets. People who live in seismically active areas will use the power of earthquakes and volcanoes. Those who live in arid regions will deify the power of dust storms and sandstorms, thunderstorms and rain.

People will also shape the Divine energy according to their culturally approved aspirations. Luck is pretty universal, while honor, inspiration to create, the ability to comprehend the universe, and romantic love will vary from culture to culture. Whatever people's needs they will find a way to make a form that will allow the Divine energy that is most pertinent to those needs to be manifested most clearly and strongly. Therefore, throughout time humans have had Mother Gods, hunter gods, farming gods, smith gods, gods of love, gods of protection, gods of childbirth, and gods of death. As their cultures evolved and become more complex, they formed gods of knowledge, gods of justice and mercy, gods of truth, and gods of lies. In some places people developed gods of music, poetry, and dance. In others, gods inhabited drums and masks. In yet other places, gods were given shape in ephemeral sand paintings. (Hermes, an ancient pre-Hellenic God-form, was a God of Thievery and Lying. His worshipers were originally pirates and found nothing wrong in either of those two acts. Whether or not Hermes actually helped them in their piracy is another matter.)

The powers of the natural universe—the sun, moon, and stars, the wind and rain, the ice and the Sea—were also made comprehensible by being shaped into gods. For while Divinity is not knowable, the forms placed upon the Divine Facets *are* knowable, and through knowledge comes understanding, growth, healing, and self-control.

I am not indicating that a human being can (or should) control an earthquake or a thunderstorm. What a human being can do is control his or her own emotional response to natural phenomena. Even more important are our responses to the fundamental human processes of birth, growth, death, and rebirth. All of these processes can be better understood and dealt with if there is a way to tap into the Divine energy behind them. Accordingly, what I mean by a God-form is the humanly made and defined shape through which a particular aspect of Divinity is made comprehensible to the human mind.

God-forms can be male, female, or hermaphroditic. They can be heterosexual, homosexual, or bisexual. (There are even some asexual or genderless gods. Most of them are the abstract and impersonal creations of priesthoods or philosophers.)

God-forms can be young, middle-aged, or old, or can have several aspects, as in the Celtic Maiden-Mother-Crone God-form. In whatever way you may discover Them, They are what Their peoples needed Them to be.

3

Considerations of Evil

ೞ

At this point it seems appropriate to deal with the idea of an evil God-form. Our cultural heritage has given many people the idea that, if they set out to invoke or evoke a God-form, they may find themselves possessed by a demon, or face-to-face with one.

I do not believe that such a thing can exist. Divinity is Love. Evil is a refusal to love. Divinity is healing, happiness, and progress. Evil is wanting not to heal, wanting not to be happy, and desiring to stagnate. Therefore, demons and evil God-forms are impossibilities.

This is not to deny that evil exists. It does, and it comes from human behavior. Whatever "demons" are in your mind and culture, they were put there by human beings, their dysfunctions, and abusive practices. Dealing with the manifestations and residues of human evil is unfortunately a necessary part of the practice of invocation and evocation, as we will see in the following chapters, but there is no superhuman evil to worry about.

In saying this, I am aware that I am contradicting those religions that posit an evil God-form. For example, most forms of Christianity, the belief system in which I was raised, hold that there is a Devil. The Devil is a perfect example of an evil God-form. (Christians usually deny that the Devil is a God-form at all, but his independent will, godlike power, and immortality qualify him for the title. He is believed to have been created rather than creating himself, but the same is true of most of the God-forms in which human beings have believed.)

Denying the beliefs of other religions is an uncomfortable position. Our mainstream culture, at least in America, teaches us that it is bad to criticize other people's religions. There are good reasons for this, because the religious disagreements of the past 2000 years have fueled countless bloody persecutions, pogroms, and wars. However, in many countries, the acceptance of the principle of freedom of religion means that religious disagreements can be peaceful. They don't have to be fought until the winners take over the government and persecute the losers, so it is not necessary to consider criticism of a religious belief the opening shot of a religious war. Certainly, my interpretation of Paganism holds that it is wrong even to proselytize, let alone persecute. If I contradict some cherished beliefs of some other religions, I hope that we can all agree to disagree.

I need to say explicitly that there are no evil God-forms, and belief in them is dangerous to anyone who seeks to practice invocation or evocation. First, it is very likely to induce enough fear to ruin any chance of success. Second, if any of the normal manifestations of all-too-human evil show up, misidentifying them as manifestations of evil Divinity can destroy one's ability to deal with them.

I will go further: It is not enough to deny the existence of evil God-forms, as do many modern liberal Christians who have rejected the Devil. The problem is that evil God-forms are not just a mistake, nor a priestly plot to scare the faithful into obedience. When the good god-form is held to include only goodness and perfection with no trace of negativity, belief in an evil God-form naturally develops from the belief in the good God-form.

Any "perfect" God-form must be unique, absolutely outside of the Universe, and distinct from it. An evil God-form then arises as a sort of negative spiritual after-image, and serves as the repository for those aspects of Divinity and Earthly reality that will not cohere with the "perfect" goodness of the good god-form, aspects such as death, pain, and suffering. In many belief systems, the good and evil god-form are thought of as being in conflict with one another, with humans caught in the middle. This is the pattern followed by most of the world's major religions. Even most "mystical" religions fit the pattern: they tend to posit an impersonal, formless, blissful Divinity, and an equally impersonal, formless, miserable Illusion that keeps human beings from knowing this bliss.

Religions with transcendent god-forms have another, related problem of evil that is even more fundamental than the tendency to believe in evil god-forms. All such religions I am aware of believe that, although the physical universe has been created or manifested by the "perfect" transcendent God-form, it is in some way worthless, base, or even evil. Consequently, human beings must deny, resist, transcend, or abandon it. And here the circle closes. Humans are part of the universe, with no prospect of escape but death—if through that—so when the universe is devalued they are inevitably devalued along with it.

This is a bitter historical irony. Transcendent God-forms were surely created to give shape to people's yearnings for a better life for themselves and their children. In hard and violent times, it may have seemed that a God-form Who could improve human life would have to overcome the whole world. Perhaps this is why these God-forms came to be imagined as outside the world, transcendent. But once this was imagined a chasm opened up between the human and the Divine. After that, the process of crediting the God-form with more and more goodness and power began to subtract value from the world and the people in it.

In many such belief systems, humans by now, are left with no intrinsic value; they have only whatever value the transcendent

God-form may choose to grant them or what merit they may gain from worshiping Him. Some systems even hold that human beings are all born condemned to eternal punishment unless and until they are redeemed by special, unmerited Divine favor.

To be sure, these statements represent my own summary of some of the official higher theology of such systems. Many religious leaders, and many more believers, would disagree that their religion actually teaches such things. And it is true that most organized religions are gradually moving away from such harsh views. Nevertheless, such principles were considered fundamental in the recent past. They still have many supporters; they still permeate many sermons and prayers; and subconsciously at least, they still have an effect.

The effect is not a good one. These beliefs are tragically dysfunctional. People who despise themselves, their human nature, and the fact of their own existence are more likely to abuse and harm others. They are less likely to make the best of what they have. They are far less likely to be able to experience Divinity. They have been spiritually crippled, and, in my opinion, the belief systems that impose this crippling are spiritually abusive.

After over twenty-five years of studying the doctrines of the major religions, I am convinced that there is no transcendent perfect god-form, and no evil God-forms either. My experience, and that of many other mystics, shows the contrary. The Universe itself is Divine. It contains everything and nothing. The Universe is a self-aware, self-creating Divinity. It and its laws are functional. It does not deny itself or hold itself apart from itself. It is therefore incapable of being evil.

My experience of the Gods is that they value us as they value themselves. There are two sides to this:

1. The Gods respect us. They will never deny us the results of the choices we have made and the actions we have taken. They do not interfere in our lives. They do not expect us to obey

arbitrary "laws" such as those that tell us what to eat, whom to marry, or when to have sex. They will *never* ask us to do something that harms other humans, such as beat a child, mutilate a baby, sacrifice a living person to them, kill another in their name, or wage a war for their glory.

2. The Gods respect one another. They do not deny one another's existence, for They are all facets of the same Divinity.

4

From Whence the
Nightmares Come

∞

When you invoke or evoke, you can be certain that there are no
Divine powers that will take control of you without your
consent. The powers that you do invite in will not ask you to do
evil things. Further, you are always the one who has the final
authority, and nice as it might be to shed the responsibility of
your actions, you cannot give the control of your actions and the
consequences of those actions over the God-forms in such a way
that you are simply a tool.

However, you need to be aware that your own past abuse
issues can come up during invocation and evocation. Many
people, and I would say most people, have these issues. They
originate in real abuse: the monstrous pain and terror that
people have been subjected to as children, whether regularly or
only occasionally. It is possible to repress or displace the memory
of such events completely. It is also possible to remember the
events as facts, without recalling the feelings from the events.
Many of us have protected ourselves in these ways.

As a result of the energy flows of invocation and evocation, these memories can surface unexpectedly and powerfully. If you are not aware of what they mean, they can be very frightening. They can seem to take over, and that can be a terrifying event. It may even seem as though an altogether different "person" is talking to you, telling you things that seem unbelievable, urging you to act in ways that are counterproductive or dysfunctional. A good portion of this book therefore deals with ways to avoid being overwhelmed by such memories—the forgotten tapes that can run (and ruin) your life.

Once you know where the bad memories are and what they are about, they can no longer terrify you. They can make you sad and angry, but they will not feel that something or someone other than yourself is intruding into your invocation or evocation rituals, or running your life.

If such memories surface, one of the first things to do is seek the assistance of a qualified therapist. This book is not a substitute. I believe that no therapist except one trained to deal with posttraumatic stress syndrome will be effective. However, that is my personal, nonprofessional opinion. As always, find out for yourself.

Second, always be aware that everyone has frightening memories that for a wide variety of reasons have been buried. For instance, there are very few people who have not been frightened by horror movies, or have not enjoyed having their wits scrambled by a good gothic suspense novel. But the images in the movies and books, as well as other communication media, are directly derived from real abuse, harm, and terror. So when one is learning to invoke and evoke, it is important to become very clear about what the real memories are and what are the "special effects." That is a good rule to keep in mind with regard to the positive effects of invocation and evocation as well. Very little is as the Screen Artists Guild portrays it, as delightful or horrifying as that might be.

5

Creating the Sacred Space
Within Yourself

ဢ

The space in which an invocation or evocation is performed plays an important role in determining whether what appears within it will be real or imaginary. If the space is secure and powerful, then very little of the horrific memories or the fanciful make-believe will intrude. On the other hand, if the space is created haphazardly or with inappropriate intent, then little of what occurs within it can be relied upon to be valid. The memories, repressed emotions, and all the special effects of television and cinema will be much more likely to show up. Therefore, it is vitally important to create the sacred space with careful intention and focus.

A sacred space is any area of emotional or physical and temporal space that is being set aside, prepared for, and used for a sacred intention. The most important sacred space, and the one that we shall first work on developing, is the space inside you. Obviously, if you are going to invite a facet of Divinity into yourself, you want the "room" to be clean, pretty, and not cluttered with junk.

This chapter contains five ritual meditations and magickal workings that will provide valuable assistance in creating your internal sacred space. Please practice each one, and if you find yourself getting impatient, remember that this kind of discipline takes time and dedication to master. Let us begin with a simple clearing.

Meditation 1: Cleaning Your Personal House

This meditation is useful even when you are not preparing to invoke or evoke Divinity. It can be of great assistance when trying to clear your mind for an exam, test, or interview, or when you have to deal with an unpleasant or emotionally charged situation.

Sit in an upright chair with your back straight and legs uncrossed, your hands relaxed in your lap. Or, stand with your back straight, your hands relaxed at your sides, and your knees unlocked (you will have to direct a specific thought to your knees to get them to do this and still support you).

Become aware of how your hands feel. At first they will most likely feel tight and achy. Intend them to release their tightness into the universe and slowly begin to feel warm and soothed.

Take a deep slow breath through your mouth and direct the energy of the breath into your hands. It helps to imagine the energy of your breath as having a warm color, like yellow. As you take another deep slow breath, push the color into your hands and into your fingers, and feel them getting warm. Take a third deep breath and feel the tingling sensation flow through your arms and hands. Now, with the fourth deep breath, the yellow light and the warm tingles explode with a rush into all the rest of your body, especially your chest and abdomen.

Take several normal breaths and just "be" with the light. Now, imagine you can see into your body. Floating in the light, you "see" several (or many) brown blobs. These are your worries, anxieties, angers, unresolved griefs, and frights. Let the blobs bump into one another and stick to each other. Do this until there are a reasonable number of groups, about four or five. Then, one by one, let the blobs float up out of your thoracic cavity and into your hands.

As the blobs reach your hands, imagine that they are turning into hard rocklike objects. Hold each one. Name it by remembering what it signifies, how it made you feel, and what you did in response to that feeling. Now, physically moving your arm, fling the solid blob away from you—far away from you. Give it back to the universe so that the energy contained within it, energy that was dysfunctional to you, can be decomposed and used for something else, something beautiful.

Do this with each blob. Sometimes a blob wants to return. This means that it was not sufficiently named or acknowledged. Rename it, reacknowledge it, and fling it away once more.

When all the blobs are gone, take several deep slow breaths and relax in the clear yellow glow that fills you.

Meditation 2: Comforting the Inner Child

This is a lengthy ritual that requires a long list of materials. It is one of the most powerful transformation rituals that I know. Read it through carefully several times before you actually get started.

Sometimes the blobs won't go away, no matter what you do, or how often. Sometimes, instead of brown blobs, or along with the blobs, there are ugly dead blackish-red areas. These look a lot like big scabs and seem attached to your insides. These are psychic manifestations of trauma, usually caused by real abuse. Dealing with these takes a long time and strong commitment. I have found that in cases like this, making a self-healing poppet is one of the best magickal tacks to take. Here is a method I use all the time with my coven.

Gather all the materials before you start. Do the Cleaning Your Personal House Meditation and get rid of everything that you can. Then, reassure those blackish-red areas that you respect the tender areas they are protecting, but now it is time to let light and air in. It is time to heal. Say it out loud, say it into a mirror, and keep saying it even when you are experiencing pain.

Next, make a poster. Draw a rainbow (some people like a butterfly better) and write the following phrases:

> *There is nothing wrong with me. I was born healthy and normal.*
> *Something happened to me. I am not guilty. I was not responsible.*
> *What happened was then; this is now.*
> *I can heal.*
> *I survived.*

Put that in front of you where you can see it while you are making your poppet, and if necessary, repeat the words out loud until you believe them. Then put on your favorite soothing music, have a drink of cool water, and begin.

Have the following items on a work surface in front of you:

- Eighteen inches of ordinary muslin or percale—like the cloth in a pillow case. Make sure the cloth is your skin color.
- Scissors
- Needle and thread (A sewing machine helps but is not necessary.)
- About four to six ounces of polyester stuffing
- A walnut
- A heart-shaped candy
- A small red balloon, uninflated
- A few dried beans or lentils
- A small piece of chocolate (optional)
- Two small natural sponges

- A yellow marble or a yellow gumball (You might use a small clear crystal, but I think the color yellow is important.)
- A tiny piece of hot red pepper such a Thai pepper, about the size of the marble
- Twenty-nine inches of thin red yarn
- Six inches of wire or a pipe cleaner
- Two 4mm beads, the color of your eyes
- Colored pencils, crayons, markers, or paints
- A piece of colored felt that matches your skin color
- A piece of card, or thin cardboard about five inches long and three inches wide
- Embroidery floss or yarn the color of your hair
- White glue or fabric glue (I like a product called Fabric-Tac.)

1. Take the muslin or percale and cut two paper doll–shaped figures. I have included a pattern; if you use it, blow it up by 200 percent at a local copy shop.
2. Sew along all the edges. Take tiny stitches and close it up completely. Then cut a slit down the back, from right beneath the head to the groin.
3. Wrap the walnut in a bit of the stuffing and put it into the head. As you do this, say the following out loud and clearly: "I am an intelligent and creative person."
4. Stuff the face area of the head and make sure that the back and sides of the head are firmly packed.
5. Put a thin layer of stuffing on the very front of the chest and abdominal areas. Wrap the candy heart in a bit of stuffing and put it into the chest cavity, saying: "I am courageous, loving, and kind. I have the will to heal and grow."
6. Take the balloon and put a few of the beans inside it. This represents your stomach and how you want to nourish your

Poppet Pattern

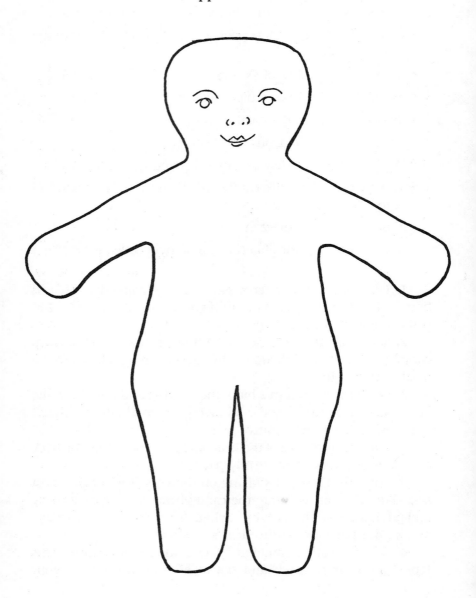

inner child on good food. (I also put a small piece of chocolate in mine, for I consider chocolate a sacred food.) Directing the words to the poppet in front of you say out loud: "I nourish myself on good food and drink. I eat only what I need. I eat to provide energy, health, and healing."

7. Wrap the sponges in a bit of stuffing and place them in the chest cavity where the lungs would be. As you do this, say: "I breathe clean air. I fill my lungs with health. I have endurance and vitality."

8. Take the twenty-nine inches of red yarn and coil it into the abdominal cavity. These represent your intestines. As you do this, say: "I take only what I need from the universe. I give back what is unnecessary or unhealthy for me."

If you wish, you can add tokens for each of the organs. You should certainly do so if you have experienced or are experiencing illness or troubles with an organ or organ system.

9. Take the yellow marble or gumball and place it just below the heart, between the lungs and behind the stomach. This is your astral center. If you are able to do so, I suggest you substitute a clear quartz crystal for this token. As you put it in place, say out loud, to yourself, to the poppet, and the entire universe: "I am a lovable and loved person. I have a right to exist in the universe. I have a right to be happy and productive."

10. Pad the chest cavity firmly but do not overpack it. Take the piece of hot pepper (which represents your sexuality) and after wrapping it in a piece of stuffing place it in the groin of the poppet. As you do so, say out loud: "I and my sexuality are holy and pure. Sex and appropriate sexual activity is fun, healing, and good for the soul. Sharing my sexuality is a good and natural act. I act responsibly. I share myself with discretion and respect the rights of others. I can say no or yes without shame!"

You may have to say this several times, for our society is obsessed with sex, making it into something that it never was or ever will be. Much, if not most, of the abuse we suffer focuses on sex and sexual actions. For millennia, people with authoritarian belief systems have tried to control others' sexuality and sexual actions. We are often told that doing what is, in fact, natural is wrong, and when the natural action is forbidden and repressed, it gets twisted and becomes something very dysfunctional— sometimes even harmful to ourselves and others. So be very careful when you work on this aspect. Let your feelings, whatever they may be, come up and express themselves as you handle your sexuality. If you feel ashamed or dirty, stop and ask yourself why. Write down what comes to mind, and holding that thought, go back to making the poppet.

11. Now, fill the legs and arms of the poppet with stuffing and put the wire or pipe cleaner in the place for the spine. As you do this, say: "I can stand on my own, I make a positive contribution to the world. I am connected."

12. Finish any stuffing and sew up the back slit. Turn the doll over and sew on the beads where the eyes should go. As you do this, say: "I can see clearly. I can see through despair and pain, fog and illusion."

13. Take the paints, pencils, crayons, or markers and draw on a nose and a smile—a pretty (or, if you prefer, handsome), confident smile. If you like your teeth, let them show. If you find it difficult to draw a smile, ask yourself why you deserve to be sad, and when the answer comes, write it down and continue. As you draw the smile, say: "I deserve to be happy, to laugh and sing. I deserve to be listened to, to have an opinion and have it respected. I have worthwhile things to say."

14. Cut out two ears from the felt and sew them in place. If you wish, draw earrings on the ears, and as you sew on the ears, say: "I can hear the truth. I can accept praise and criticism. I can listen and understand."

15. Now sew on the hair. It is easiest to take the index card and wrap the floss, thread, or yarn around it many times (at least thirty). Then sew through the middle of the card to make a part. Be sure to catch each hair as you sew. Pull the card loose from the yarn. It should be perforated in many places by the needle

and "punch out" like an old-fashioned paper doll. Now glue the yarn to the head of the poppet. Style the hair if you want, although that is not necessary, unless you have a thing about your hair. If bad-hair days are your bane, then by all means do what you need to feel good about how it looks. Glue, hair spray, or wetting and wrapping the yarn or floss around toothpicks will help you style your hair. If you have facial hair, be sure to add that, but only if you see your inner child as having it.

16. Now draw on your breasts and nipples, belly button and genitals. If your inner child has pubic hair, make sure it is there. Draw on the fingers and toes and, if you want, color your nails.

Now your poppet is complete, and you are probably out of time and exhausted. That's okay. Put the poppet under your pillow and clean up. Don't do anything with it just yet.

Wait a week, keeping the poppet under the pillow. You can say "Hi," "Good night," "Good morning," and "'Bye" to the poppet if you want, but don't do anything else for a week. This is an important time when all the internal work that you did while creating the poppet is getting connected to your inner psychic pathways. Don't stress them. Let the connection happen slowly and naturally.

After a week, take the poppet out and tell it its name. Carefully listen to yourself and see if you get an argument. Find out if the poppet already has a name. Don't argue with the poppet, respect its wishes. (Remember, the poppet is a representation of your psychic child in the physical world and deserves complete respect.)

Name the poppet. Talk to it, telling it how much you love him or her. Tell her how sorry you are that all those bad things happened, but that you will take care of him and never let them happen again.

At this point, expect to get an argument, and I mean big time. You may find yourself screaming that you haven't protected her, that you always let her down, and so on. Let those screams and yells come up. There is a lot of hurt and dysfunctional energy behind them that needs to be released. Listen to those accusations. Do not argue with them—they are probably true in one sense or another—but then look at your poster (remember the poster?) and say the words, out loud, to the poppet:

> *There is nothing wrong with me. I was born healthy and normal.*
> *Something happened to me. I am not guilty. I was not responsible.*
> *What happened was then, and this is now.*
> *I can heal.*
> *I survived.*

Now add:

> *And so did you!*

Most people find that this precipitates a good cry. Let it happen. If you need to break some dishes, do it. It's cheaper and cleaner than breaking your body with illnesses. Secondhand shops sell therapeutic crockery cheap.

Start to talk to the poppet as often as you can. Listen to what the poppet says in return. Perhaps you will make or buy your poppet some clothing or jewelry. When you are ready, sit down, do Meditation 1, then, holding the poppet with the tenderness and care that a mother would hold her newborn, tell it how much you love it and how much you need him or her to love you. Then ask the poppet to tell you what happened. Ask the poppet who or what made the big blackish-red scabs inside of you.

Trust what the poppet tells you. The inner child does not lie! Sometimes, however, he or she uses symbols to communicate. Respect those symbols, but understand that they may need to be taken figuratively and not literally. Having the poppet say you were eaten by a bear does not necessarily mean that you are remembering a past life. For example, it could mean that someone big, powerful, and angry acted aggressively against you. Here again, you must be very careful to weed out the Hollywood special effects. Let the bizarre images float, but do not dismiss them. They are most likely symbols, but in a few rare cases they may be real.

Keep a diary of what the poppet says. Watch for patterns to develop. Notice the different events and ideas that the poppet is interested in, what does it fear or hate? Ask the poppet to write you letters and offer to hold the pen and spell the words.

If you find yourself recalling vivid emotional images, they are most likely real flashbacks to abusive incidents. Write them down and share them with your therapist. Real memories are always accompanied by emotions, although not always appropriate ones. I know a young woman who has feelings of intense humor when remembering some pretty bad physical abuse.

Not every memory will be visual. Remember, you may have had your eyes closed, or you may have been face down and unable to see what was happening. Trust your feelings.

There is no need to hurry this process. It will take a long time, and everyone has a different level of tolerance. But as you do the Cleaning Your Personal House Meditation, you will soon see the "scabs" starting to break free and float up, solidifying so that you can fling them away along with the brown blobs.

Now I want to be very clear that when you do this, you are not flinging away the memories of the abusive incidents. What you are doing is ridding yourself, for a while, of the dysfunctional feelings and actions that those memories hold. You will never be rid of the memories, nor should you want to be, for you gained strength and courage by living through those times. What you don't need anymore is pain, dysfunction, and unhealthy behaviors.

Meditation 3: Taking Out the Garbage

As important as getting a clear idea of what the ugly underlying memories may be is handling the daily crud, the ordinary psychic garbage of our lives.

Daily crud is the ongoing unease or distress caused by the frictions of daily life. There is no way to avoid most of it. Traffic jams will happen; trains will be missed. But this kind of emotional scum mustn't be brought into the sacred space with you. Happily, it is more easily dealt with than the deeply buried damage. Here is what to do:

First, get a brown bag and some cheap paper, the cheaper the better—you don't want to give the daily crud too much importance.

Second, write the numbers 1 through 20 on the paper, and then write down an annoyance, irritation, anger, grudge, sadness, or peeve—you can think of that many, I am certain—next to the numbers. Make sure you get at least twenty.

Third, crush the pieces of paper tightly in your hand, and enjoy the sensation of crumpling those items of daily crud up in your fist. Really feel the release that comes with not letting them run your life.

Fourth, as you crumple each one, stick it in the bag. When the bag is full (or you have run out of daily crud) take out the garbage—literally. Drop your troubles in the trash dumpster.

Meditation 4: Opening the Rose

This meditation is helpful in opening the sacred space within yourself. It is one of the first of the invoking meditations, and it is the first sacred space you will need to learn to create. It is simple, takes little time, and you probably already know how to do it.

1. Decide which one of the following you wish to work with first:

Healing
Acceptance
Trust
Knowledge

You will need to work with all of them, but make sure you deal with each one at a separate time.

2. Sit in a comfortable position, either in a chair or on the floor. *Do not lie down.* You will go to sleep if you do.

3. Imagine a rosy glow in a spot directly beneath your sternum. Imagine that the spot is about the size of a walnut.

4. Feel the warmth of the spot.

5. Now, "see" that spot turn into a rose bud. (It can be any color of rose you desire, but I have found that it is most effective if the color is natural for roses. It is hard for the mind to accept the reality of a blue or black rose.)

6. Lift your arms so they cross your chest and your hands are on your opposite shoulders. Tense your arms until they *almost* hurt. Don't push to the point of pain; pain is harmful to these meditations, as are fasting and other ascetic practices.

7. Release the tension and let your arms slowly relax back down toward your sides. As they relax, allow the rose to bloom, to open. As it opens, you will feel a warmth entering your body from behind your left shoulder. Accept this warmth. Do not question it, rationalize it, or reason it away. If you do, it will realize that it is not welcome and leave.

8. Very important: Name the warmth. If you decided to work with healing, say out loud, "I name you Healing." (If you prefer to speak in archaic terms to further define the sacredness of what you are doing, you can use *thee* and *thou*. Just be aware that long ago these were informal, everyday usages and *you* and *your* were formal, dignified usages.)

9. Now, let Healing bloom in the rose. The center of the rose will become transparent. After doing this meditation three or four times, you will probably find yourself "hearing" something when the center of the rose becomes transparent. It may be a tone, a whisper, or even a word. Accept the message. Even if you do not understand it now, you will understand it later. Write it down in your magickal journal.

10. The first few times you do this meditation, allow yourself to be with the rose for about ten to fifteen minutes, then increase the time of just "being" with the rose so that you can ultimately be in the center of the rose for an hour or so. (By "just 'being' with the Rose," I mean that you do nothing. Allow whatever thoughts that happen to enter your mind to do so. Acknowledge them and let them pass through, but make sure that they pass through the rose. At first you will have a lot of free associations, worries, and distractions. That is perfectly normal. Just make sure these enter and leave through the rose.)

11. After you have been with the rose, allow it to close, letting the warmth leave through the bottom of your feet. Take several deep breaths and give yourself a hug. (Hugs are very good for grounding.) Now stretch your muscles and get something healthy to eat, with high protein and high grain. It doesn't have to be much, but something.

Repeat this process until you have dealt with healing, acceptance, trust, and knowledge.

At least at first, you will find that doing these meditations and exercises may feel draining, that they seem to take more energy than they give. Learning new things, opening new neural and psychic pathways, takes energy. As in priming a pump or starting an engine, at first you have to put in energy to get much more energy out later. I am going to close this chapter with a short meditation that will help you recharge your psychic batteries.

Meditation 5: Recharge!

This is a good meditation to do every morning when you wake up.

1. Take in four deep slow breaths.
2. On the fourth breath, "see" a yellow light entering your left hand and exiting through your right hand.

3. Take three more breaths, seeing the light entering your left hand and exiting through your right hand.

4. On the next breath, see a bright light forming directly under your sternum (breastbone), about the size of a pea.

5. Continue to take deep slow breaths, and gradually enlarge the size of the light from pea to marble, to acorn, to walnut, to lemon, and finally to the size of a grapefruit.

6. When the light is the size of a grapefruit, it will seem to fill your entire chest and you will feel its warmth.

7. Make a conscious decision that on the next breath, the light will suddenly expand to fill your entire body, and that with it you will have a *shan'da* (an amount beyond understanding) of energy.

8. Take that breath, feel the energy explode through your body, and get up. You will have more than enough energy to do your daily work and meditations (unless of course you have a physical illness or condition, in which case most of the energy will be directed toward correcting that condition).

6

Creating the Physical Sacred Space Around You

ကၢ

Let's turn our attention to creating the sacred space in the external physical world. As important as the internal space is, without the supporting external space it is fragile and unprotected.

A sacred space does not have to be a circle of people dressed in pseudo-archaic robes in a dark room with lit candles and clouds of incense smoke. Those props are nice and can be very conducive to the process of invocation and evocation, but they are not necessary. Unlike some authors on Wicca and Witchcraeft, I will not tell you that you need to have a specifically colored candle with a matching set of anointing oils (one for the candle and one for you), nor will I do more than suggest what I have found to be helpful. The truth is that sacred space can be created anywhere, and with no props whatsoever, if the will and intention of the person creating the space are strong enough.

There are, however, many places that are inhospitable to the creation of sacred space. I know a woman who created an elaborate ritual in a maximum-security prison. The ritual may have been successful, but the cost to the woman was severe mental upset and physical distress. Such a place contains strong negative energies that make it extremely difficult to create the secure and potent energy wall that is so necessary for invocation and evocation.

It is also very difficult to create sacred space in places where there are a great many other stimuli overwhelming the senses. I know a group that tried to have a ritual in the middle of a shopping mall. The results were disastrous. The people in the group were flooded with the anxiety and distress that runs rampant through shopping malls.

Whatever the setting, it should be relatively secure: a place that will not have uninvolved people moving in or out; a place where the music, drumming, or singing of the group will not cause distress or curiosity in others. Gardens, parks, museums, forests, wilderness areas, and backyards are wonderful locations for creating sacred spaces, as long as you can make them secure from other people. However, few of us have safe spaces in the exterior world, places where no strangers will wander by, where we can have bonfires, drum and chant, throw ourselves about in the ecstasy of invocation and evocation, and not attract attention. If you do possess such a refuge, by all means use it! But since almost all of us must share our outdoors with others—many of whom are not Pagan-friendly—this unfortunately rules out using the outdoors for anything but the simplest workings. Unless you have a couple of hundred acres, the nosy neighbors staring over your fence can finish off your ritual before you even get it going.

Therefore, this chapter will focus on indoor spaces, where doors can be locked and windows shut. Kitchens, living rooms, and bedrooms are all good places, depending on the intention of your ritual. I have done some really powerful work in a garage. The bathroom is one of the best places for solitary rituals. Why? Because even if there is no security or safety anywhere else in our lives, most of us are able to have privacy, and therefore feel safe, in the bathroom.

If you are doing a ritual in an apartment with paper-thin walls, make sure that all noise is kept to a minimum. It is better to whisper than to have an angry neighbor bang on the wall during a loudly chanted invocation.

Hanging the walls with cloth will absorb a lot of sound. Cheap fuzzy foam-based blankets are effective, colorful, and easily washed. You can even paint on them with ordinary acrylic paints. Be sure to have the windows covered.

As to the rest of the ritual setting, make it as pleasing to the eye as possible. I suppose one could do an invocation in a filthy mess, but would you really want to invite Divinity into a place like that? Normal cleanliness is adequate.

Remove all excess furniture. Sweep or vacuum the floors with a focused intention of clearing away bad energy, and light a few candles in safe places where they won't be knocked over. If you are using a draped area, put the candles in jars. People often move suddenly and vigorously in the course of invocation and evocation, and knocking over candles is not a part of the ritual, nor is putting out a fire.

It is not necessary to have an altar, but if you feel better with one, by all means use it. It is extremely helpful to mark the floor in some temporary manner to delineate the boundaries of the sacred space. Chalk and reflective tape work well on carpet. I know several groups who have exquisitely carved and decorated pieces of wood that define the arc of the circle, and one group that holds the wooden pieces in place with Velcro. Technology is a wonderful thing; use it with imagination.

Images and symbols of the God-forms with Whom you intend to work can be placed around the circle, on the altar, or in the middle of the space. Don't put anything fragile or extremely precious in the circle; worrying about it will distract you.

If you use incense, use it sparingly. The same goes for anointing oils. While the sense of smell is a very powerful aid, do not overwhelm yourself or create a breathing hazard. It is extremely difficult to conduct a successful evocation or invocation with your eyes streaming and your lungs burning from an overpowering scent.

Here is a tip from a very magickal person, Christopher Hatton, who taught me one of the most powerful evocation rituals I know: use the same scent every time you invoke or evoke a specific God-form. After a while the scent, by itself, will move you into a sacred trance state, and the invocation and evocation will just flow from your magickal consciousness.

Try not to use a scent that you will run into in the mundane world. Imagine your chagrin if you are used to using coconut incense and oil to invoke Aphrodite and then find yourself manifesting the Goddess of Love and Passion when your Aunt Mabel serves you macaroons or coconut custard pie!

The aural setting is important too. You have taken care of sound bothering your neighbors; now make sure that the music or drumming you and your group are using is suitable. Keep the music simple. Elaborate chants, complex musical scores, and many-versed songs are not conducive to the trance state necessary for a successful invocation or evocation. It is best to use repetitive chants with few words and a simple tune. Drumming without words is extremely powerful and is my background music of choice, although I once led a group invocation to a score by ELO. The music worked with what we were doing and the ritual was very powerful and satisfying.

Finally, have something to eat and drink after the main part of the ritual is completed, but while you are still in the sacred space. Whole grains and fruit juice are excellent. This is important, for nothing else is quite as grounding as eating.

What it all comes down to is this: outside or inside, plan ahead.

For your physical setting, be sure you have:

- A setting that is secure from intrusion
- A clean space, freshly swept with the expressed intention of removing negative energies

- Little or no furniture
- The sacred space marked on the floor, defining its boundaries
- Walls and windows draped, if possible
- Candles in secure holders and in safe places
- Moderate amounts of incense and oil
- Appropriate symbols and decorations
- Something simple and wholesome to eat and drink after the ritual

7

Psychic First Aid

ℒℴℭ

When you have worked to create sacred space inside you and a protected ritual space outside, you then need to consider the emotional and psychic space that is formed by the people with whom you are working. One of the most difficult things to provide for is the impact that other people will have on you, your magick, and the invocation. For as much as we would like to feel that we are in total control of the situation, the truth is other people are the single most common cause of invocations and evocations not succeeding.

You probably won't be able to recognize in advance the person or persons who will cause you the worst problems. Until they are staring you in the face, with their fangs bloody and their games played, they will seem like good friends, supportive acquaintances, and even your lovers. I do not mean to indicate that these people are inherently evil; they are not. They are simply people who have not dealt with their abuse issues and are seeking some sort of solace out of the souls of other people. Few of these people have the slightest idea of what they are doing or their effects on others' magickal work.

While it is almost impossible to prevent these people from

damaging you, your group, and your ritual, at least the first time you encounter them, there are certain steps that you can take to help you survive their attacks. Before I go any further, let me define two terms that I use in my teachings. When I use the word *fried* I am referring to the consequences of having too much energy loaded into your system too quickly, having hostile or angry energy contaminate the incoming energy, or being unexpectedly cut off from the energy source by an outside disruption.

The feeling of being fried is exactly that—you feel burned all over, as though you had somehow been sunburned on all your nerve endings. An especially bad fry can make you feel like your entire body, inside and out, has been seared with hot steam. Headaches, body shakes, muscle tremors, nausea, and intestinal distress may result. Although there are many things that can and must be done to treat a fry, it is better to avoid one in the first place.

When I use the term *iced,* I am referring to the condition in which you have opened up and nothing or very little happens (or appears to have happened—more on that later). This can be caused by insufficient preparation, but is most likely caused by outside interference, the most common of which is, again, from other people: skeptics, antagonists, or people who are using mind-altering substances in the vicinity of the ritual.

Being iced usually feels as though you have suddenly stepped off the end of a staircase expecting another step, but there is none. You psychically stumble. Depending on the degree of disruption and interference, it can also feel as though you have fallen into a pit, that you are freezing cold (hence the term *iced*), that you have the shakes, tingling sensations in your extremities, numbness in your fingers and toes, and a sudden headache. At its worst, you feel as though you have a vampire or energy leech attached to you, draining your life away, and in those cases, that is very likely what has happened.

As I mentioned, other people are the single most common

cause of invocations and evocations not succeeding. In the magickal community, we often find ourselves working with people who have "a full six-pack but lack the plastic thingy to hold it all together" (author unknown). Worse, we sometimes come across people who are so badly damaged that they have belief systems that require them to prey on other people.

It has always amazed me that the archetype of the vampire is so often thought to be glamorous and powerful. In reality, these people are the most pathetic, helpless, useless, powerless, weak, and ineffective individuals. They can do nothing for themselves, having to obtain the very simplest energies and abilities from others. Unable to be in the most ordinary relationships without causing damage, in a magickal relationship they are black holes into which unlimited amounts of energy will flow unreciprocated if not prevented. Vampires, energy leeches, and other power-suckers must be kept out of your life at all costs!

Keeping them away is a priority, for they are attracted to healthy, powerful people the way moths are attracted to light. Becoming aware of the games they play, the tactics they use to ensnare others, and the abuses that they dump into relationships must be an ongoing and continuous part of your magickal life. For they are a fact of life in the world at large, and in the magickal community in particular. Don't feel sorry for them— that only buys into their game—and don't try to help them, for that keeps them helpless. If you find yourself getting a thrill out of trying to fix things for them, you are already involved in the enabling cycle and probably need professional help to extricate yourself. Groups that deal with Adult Children Of Alcoholics (commonly known as ACOAs) are especially helpful.

So, how do you prevent yourself from being "iced"? Avoid vampires, and don't do invocations or evocations around hostile people or people who are standing back, withholding their own energies and maintaining a "show-me" attitude. In these situations, you cannot trust—you dare *not* trust. If, for some reason, you are not aware that you have possible outside interference and do get fried or iced, here is the most basic and necessary psychic first aid.

First: Do not wait to finish the ritual. LEAVE! Let other people worry about the disruption to the circle. The first rule of the Craeft is "take care of yourself," and this is a situation that is a very good place to practice it. Have someone you trust get you to a safe place where others, even well-meaning others, cannot intrude on you. I suggest a bathroom with a door that can be locked. This is *very* important in the case of vampires and leeches, for once they have attached themselves they really do not want the connection broken and will flock around, offering what seems to be help but is in reality only the desire to feed some more. Putting a physical barrier between yourself and the disruption is essential. If you have no one you can trust, trust your wise self and get yourself to a safe place.

Second: Drink some water. Do *not* drink teas or herbs, sugar or caffeine. Do not take homeopathic "cures," and absolutely do not drink anything alcoholic. Water is the miracle healer, especially for psychic problems. Drink about eight ounces slowly. Sip it and you will feel the heat of the fry or the cold of the ice easing.

Third: Rub yourself all over with the flat of your hands, or if you have a trusted friend with you, have him or her rub you. Make sure that every square millimeter of your body gets rubbed (rub the middle of your back on a door jamb or piece of furniture). It is not necessary to remove your clothing to do this—the rubbing works just as well through cloth. And I do mean every square millimeter: Your scalp, between your toes, your genitals, inside your ears and nose. Concentrate especially on your hands and fingers, nose, lips, and the area around your navel. Rub for several minutes, firmly yet gently. Do not abrade your skin. Pay attention to that, for you may find yourself wanting to "scrub" yourself raw. Touch yourself the way you would touch a newborn infant, with care and respect.

Fourth: When you can stand without shaking, do so, and

close your eyes. "See" a cord of bright blue light running up out of the floor (ground) where you stand, becoming your spine and exiting out the crown of your head. Just be with that blue light for a few moments, then slowly wrap yourself in the light as though it were a big piece of plastic wrap. Use only what you need and let the rest of the light go.

Fifth: rejoin the ritual, but this time notice who is trying to dig a hole through your "wrapping." These people are most likely the ones who caused interference in the first place. Only the most dedicated leeches and power-suckers will keep trying to feed off you.

At this point, what is of more concern are the angry or scoffing skeptics. These people need to be confronted and asked to leave (or if you are on their turf, you need to leave). If it is not possible to remove the interfering person or persons and you cannot leave, *do not continue with the ritual.*

The person or persons who have caused the interference will most likely respond with an angry or tolerantly amused denial that they did anything; indeed, they won't see what the fuss is all about. After all, nothing was happening; they weren't experiencing anything—ad nauseam. And that's what caused the problem: their own internal barriers, psychic jamming, and intense disbelief.

Don't attempt to reason with or convert these people. They have closed belief systems and will explain everything away in terms of their closed belief systems (somewhat in the way right-wing Christians explain away any historical evidence that contradicts their beliefs by saying that the Devil created the evidence to cast doubt on their faith). It is a waste of your time and energy trying to talk to these people and you have better things to do, like figuring out how not to have them in your life anymore.

To recap the psychic first-aid measures:

- *Other people are the single most common cause of invocations and evocations not succeeding.*

- Do not wait to finish the ritual. LEAVE! Get to a safe space, preferably one with a door that can be locked. If possible, have someone you trust with you.
- Drink eight ounces of plain water.
- Rub yourself all over with the flat of your hands. If you have someone with you, let him or her help with hard-to-reach spots.
- Wrap yourself in a protective sheet of blue light. At this point it may be hard to achieve a trance, so just imagine or pretend that you have done so. It will work.
- Rejoin the ritual and have the person or persons responsible for the interference removed. If this is not possible, *do not* continue with the ritual.

PART II

≉S≈

Invocation

8

Preparation for Invocation

Samhain, 1995

The woman lights a single candle and sits back in her chair. Downstairs she can hear the sounds of the group gathering, the social chatter, the bustle of people coming and going. It seems so very far away, so removed from the flickering flame. She watches the flame for a moment, and then as she starts to slip into trance, she runs through her preritual preparatory list.

She calls up the face and the name of each participant in tonight's ritual. She makes a judgment on why they are there, what they need, what their limitations and tolerances are, and what is the worst-case scenario if the ritual is too "hot" or too "cold" for them. She decides that all of the people are in a positive emotional space, with the exception of a young man who has just been diagnosed HIV positive. He may not be able to handle the full force of the invocation. She decides to "loop him out" of the ritual's energies.

Finishing with the group, she turns to herself. She recalls all of the irritations, anxieties, and worries that have plagued her in the last week. She creates mental images of them as brown pieces of paper, and then she imagines that she is crumpling the paper into small balls and tossing them away. Far away.

Then she looks at what she wants from the ritual and from the invocation. She considers the various God-forms with Whom she has worked in the past. She decides on an appropriate locus of connection, and a Persona. She decides on a method. Finally, she is finished. She stands and pinches the candle out. She is not surprised that the noise and commotion downstairs has vanished, that the group is gathered in silence, waiting for her. It is time. Time to dance with Divinity.

This woman is an accomplished practitioner of the art of invocation and a priestess. She has taken care that the ritual will be as positive and as empowering as possible, for herself and the other participants. Let us look at what she did in an analytical light. She made a mental list. If she were involved with a larger group containing people who were new to the Craeft, unfamiliar to her, or especially needy, she might have made a written list. She considered each person as a special individual with unique characteristics and needs. Based on her past experience and on her wise self, she made a decision as to how she was going to handle each one if the energy became too intense (too hot) or if the energy failed to manifest (was too cold) for that person. She came to the decision that one person was not going to be able to handle any kind of energy at that time (except perhaps the energy of acceptance), and therefore she deliberately decided to put a mental and emotional barrier between that person and the invoked energies. She did not, however, decide to ask him to leave or to sit out the ritual.

She then used a mental technique that allowed her to step away from the daily garbage of her life. This was an important step. No one in the process of invocation can afford to have their emotional landscape littered with emotional rubbish.

Finally, she set some goals for herself so that she would be both empowered by the ritual and confirmed by the manifestation of energy. She knew that it was vital to anchor her art of magick in reality, i.e., to have a definite set of experiences occur that would signal that she had successfully accomplished what she set out to do. Her goal was to open a part of her emotional and mental "mind" so that energy originating from the Divine could enter her, speak with her mouth, see with her eyes, and heal with her hands. She wished to make the unknowable known to the others in the group, to summon forth sacred insight, and to be in an intimate contact with the Universe.

To that effect, she made conscious decisions on the specific humanized, and therefore humanly comprehensible, God-form that would best suit the needs of her group and her own personal needs. She did this in full knowledge that some other god-form could very well show up instead. But from many years of successful invocation, the priestess was confident that whichever God-form did manifest would be the most appropriate and meaningful Aspect of Divinity for the ritual.

9

Choosing an Appropriate
God-Form

ʂᴏɔ

This chapter deals with the practice of solitary invocation and
the finished product. The process starts with the act of choosing
an appropriate God-form.

It is important that you work, at least at first, with a God-form
with Whom you are comfortable and Who plays a healing and
functional role in your life. Try to stay within the framework of a
single myth system that is compatible with your life and your
magickal goals.

It is also magickally important to have a deep understanding
of the context which gave rise to the God-form and the reality of
how It related to Its people. I have noticed that many people have
only a surface familiarity with the myth systems they use. They
get a passage or two out of some children's book on myths and
go with it. Sometimes they read a modern interpretation of
mythology—perhaps with a psychoanalytical slant or maybe a
"world consciousness" framework—but they never really study
the texts from which those books are derived. This is like
reading a distant acquaintance's obituary and claiming that you

knew him well based on that newspaper account—even though you hardly knew him at all. When you are invoking Gods, that superficial relationship will not work.

Let me give you an example of what I mean. I have noticed that one of the most popular myth systems among modern Pagans and Wiccans is that of the ancient Egyptians. The Gods are splendid and beautiful; they are also powerful, distant, and exotic, with their animal aspects clearly emphasized. They are almost like characters in science fiction; at least that is the way the popular media and some poorly researched books on the subject make them appear. But if you plan on using Isis as your patron God-form, go and find out about Her.

It will take some digging. Sir Edmund Budge, for all his meticulous research in ancient Egyptian religion (Budge's book, *The Egyptian Book of the Dead,* is the primary source for most of the Egyptian mythology that is published), deals almost entirely with death rituals, after-death prophylactics, and talismanic magick. You will not find a great deal of information on Isis as she dealt with the lives of Her people in most of the books. I suggest reading Robert Graves's *The Golden Ass* and then doing some research as to why Graves wrote what he did. Use his bibliography. It won't be light reading, but it will be informative.

Most of the myths that are found in the popular books have been edited, redacted, twisted, chopped, or otherwise deformed to fit the needs of other, later belief systems, and most myths of Goddesses have been polluted and debased by male-supremacist cultures.

If you are going to work with Isis (or more correctly, Au-Set) you need to know that most likely She did not move into Her supreme female position in the Egyptian pantheon until late into the Middle Kingdom (1500 B.C.E.). Before that time, Hathor, Sekhmet, and Meres Geb were more important. Why? Research can tell you this, and more.

When dealing with other myth systems you will discover that Heka is not a nasty old woman, nor is Hera a jealous baby murderer. And you may even do enough digging to figure out that the Dagda is female, as is P'tah. All of this sort of research is extremely important when preparing to work with a god-form for the purposes of invocation. Because if you do not do the research and invoke a God-form such as Au-set, it means that when She really shows up you probably won't recognize Her.

In short, it is important to know your God-forms on Their own terms, not those that make you comfortable. Peel away the "Hollywood," the wishful thinking, the New Age pink bunny fluff, and really get to know Them.

The Gods deal with real-world issues. Being mad at your boyfriend is not a real-world issue; being beat up by your boyfriend is. The bank bouncing your check because you had five cents less than was necessary is not a real-world issue; not being able to find work is. Don't insult the Gods by invoking them for silly or trivial reasons, but don't hesitate to use them for serious reasons.

At this point, I think it is necessary to put in a word about doing rituals for world healing, environmental issues, peace, and other big issues. These are all very good reasons for doing magick, but *please* don't invoke Divine energy for them. The Gods are already extremely involved and don't need to be reminded of the mess we have made. A finite being such as a human (or a dolphin, for that matter) can only see a tiny piece of the tapestry of All-being, and will almost always cause more harm than good by trying to manipulate that tiny piece. Also, it is our problem. After all, we caused the overpopulation that pushed the environment beyond its carrying capacity. Scarce resources result in environmental degradation, war, and punitive social customs, all of which are responsible for most of the really bad situations in the world today. Given that, we probably already know the solutions to those difficulties.

So, what are *good* reasons for invocation?

Healing: Either physical or emotional. If you do healing

for someone other than yourself, always get their permission first.

Prosperity: It is perfectly OK to ask for money to supply your ordinary needs in life, or to open the doors of opportunity. *Do not* ask for wealth, vast fortune, or an opportunity that you have not earned or do not deserve. Once you have asked for money, make sure that you are working to provide a way for it to come to you.

Opportunity: The space to be recognized, appreciated, and valued for the positive work that you have done and the effort and talent that you have shown.

Spiritual Growth: Asking for direction, courage, and increased intuition will probably result in some pain, but this is the pain of stretching enough to encompass the new you—it is worth it.

Relationships: This is a tricky area. It is never a good idea to ask for Divine assistance to make or force someone to love you or go to bed with you. First, it won't work. The Gods won't coerce anyone, not for Themselves, not for you. Second, the backlash of twisted energy will manifest in some very unpleasant ways. However, if you are lonely, it is perfectly okay to ask for guidance in attracting the right person, and for insight about what you should or shouldn't do. It's also perfectly ethical to ask for help in healing a relationship that you are already in, if you are willing to be the person who is going to do whatever changing needs to be done. If you can't live with that restriction, get out of the relationship before you try using Divine energy to change another person.

Truth, Dreams, and Prophecy: These are areas that often require Divine assistance, but they can be very tricky, since the answers will often come in symbolic ways.

Whatever your reason for doing an invocation, go into the ritual with your eyes wide open, your ears and heart ready to hear, but also be willing to reserve judgment and withhold action until the full ramifications of any manifestations become clear. That can take several days, or even weeks.

I once knew a young man who practiced as a solitary but often came to me for advice. In this particular situation he didn't, and I wish he would have. The man lived in a very unsavory neighborhood in an inner city. He started to have strange dreams about a "shadow" in his apartment. In a protection ritual, he invoked a God-form that deals with dreams. The God-form clearly said, "Move away quickly and with care." The young man did not stop and think; he did not consider the complex meanings of the message. Instead he panicked, threw all of his easily movable belongings into his car, and showed up on a very surprised friend's doorstep. While he was gone, vandals broke into his apartment and stole almost everything.

Since he hadn't asked his friend if he could move in before he did so, the relationship went sour. He finally moved back into his apartment, and two weeks later was mugged and seriously stabbed in the laundry room of the building.

What should he have done?

First, he needed to listen. "Move away"—not run away or flee. *Move* away. Pack up your stuff, make some plans, and move. "Quickly"—but not instantly or that very night. When a person is moving, a week or so can be very quick indeed. "With care"— don't get sloppy; don't make assumptions. Move *with care*. Also, knowing what he knew about the building, going down into the laundry room alone was foolish, that is, he did not use care or common sense. He needed to think about the ramifications and consequences of his actions, and he should have withheld action until he had a clear plan in mind.

To be fair to the God-form, this young man had a deep need to continue to be the victim in whatever soap opera drama he was currently starring. The God-form could have said just about anything and the young man would have turned it into a disaster.

10

Practice Makes Perfect

ळ

Practice is essential. After all, the more you go through the motions, the better you'll learn your lines and know where to step, and the less likely you'll get stage fright when you stand in front of an entire group and call in your favorite deity.

Having decided what God-form(s) you are going to work with as well as the purpose of your invocation, the best place to start working is in the bathroom—in the bathtub, to be precise. If you don't have a tub, the shower will work, but be aware that you will be using an awful lot of hot water that way. Clean the bathroom thoroughly, move all the old magazines out, bring in some flowers, burn a little incense, and fill the tub with warm water—but not so warm that it will put you to sleep.

Get a glass of sparkling water, preferably in a nonbreakable cup, since broken glass in the bathtub, at least while you are in it, may likely result in a blood sacrifice, and blood sacrifices are very bad ideas most of the time.

Now, do the Taking Out the Garbage Meditation (see page 27). When you have finished, get into the tub, lie back, and relax. Close your eyes and see the circle of sacred space you are creating around yourself. It is often helpful to imagine yourself floating inside of an iridescent soap bubble. Use whatever words come readily to you, or use the short casting and calling ritual that I have included at the end of this chapter.

Call the directions (East, South, West, North, and Center) or the elements (Water, Fire, Air, Earth, and Spirit) if you feel it is necessary. Then pause. Allow that most efficacious and powerful magickal tool, your imagination—your "pretender"—to take over. Imagine that you can see a glowing hollow space inside you, that you can feel the winds and waters, the fires and the solidities of stone move through that place. This can be quite humorous, but that's okay. The gods love a good laugh.

Now take a sip of the sparkling water. Let it rest on your tongue. Really, really feel the bubbles.

Now state the name of the God-form you are invoking and why. Say it out loud. Take another sip of the sparkling water and again, really feel the bubbles. Repeat the name of the God-form you are invoking and why. This time pretend that somewhere deep in the earth below you, someone lifted her head and listened. Pretend that somewhere deep in the middle of space, high above you, someone lifted Their head and listened. Ask Them to come to the place you have made for Them. (If you are invoking only one God-form, please understand that you have aroused the notice of that God-form, at once in the earth below you and in the stars beyond you.) Take another sip of water and feel the bubbles enter the hollow glowing space inside you.

Now make a real effort with your pretender and imagine that as the bubbles enter your hollow space the power of the God-form(s) is starting to coalesce within you. Imagine that the bubbling, glowing energy is filling you up. Feel the change in yourself, that slight sideways shift that moves you into trance, and go with it. Be with the "pretended" invoked God-form. Imagine Him or Her talking through you, using your mouth, your eyes, your ears.

Now, out loud, talk. Say whatever comes into your mind, and give yourself a grace period to get past "Boy, does this feel dumb!" Believe in yourself enough to know that every new thing feels a little foolish, a little clumsy at first.

When the water starts to cool, or when you start turning into a prune, thank the god-form for coming to you. Pretend that the light and energy is leaving. See a sparkling trail of energy spiraling into the heavens and into the earth below. Release the directions if you called them, and pull the energy of the sacred space back into yourself. Get out, dry off, and write down everything that happened or that you think might have happened in your journal. Don't talk about it for a day or two. Wait. Let it settle. I am willing to wager that while at first it really does feel as though you are pretending, something will be happening. And while it is happening, while you are in it—you can't notice it happening. Later, when you are not in it, you may find yourself saying, "Wow! That was different!" When you read your journal you may find that what seemed to be silly gibberish now makes a lot of sense.

Your imagination, your pretender, is one of the most powerful and effective magickal tools that exists, which is why it is downgraded, ridiculed, and made to seem a childish toy by the belief systems that want to keep you under their control. When you come to realize its power, you will find that much of what you imagine—what you "pretend"—is simply phenomena to which others have made themselves blind, deaf, and insensitive.

Simple casting and calling ritual:

Out of that which formed me, I give form.
Out of that which blessed me, I give blessings.
Out of that which releases me, I give freedom.
The circle is cast, the center holds, the sacred space is made.
For as I will it, so mote it be.
Winds that blow, Fires that burn,
Waters that flow, Stones that stand.
Guard and guide me. Be at hand.

I always create my sacred space first and then call the directions, elements, or guardians into it, but you may do it in the other order if that is more comfortable for you.

Now you are ready to start working with—invoking—a God-form. We're going the use the same meditation technique as in "Opening the Rose." (You may find it helpful to have your inner child poppet in the room with you the first time you do this—for moral support now and for a focus of loving criticism later.)

Light a candle and feel yourself anchored to the floor. Take three deep breaths, letting them out slowly. Now place your hands over your heart and take another three deep breaths. This time, as you let the breaths out, vocalize the name of the god-form with whom you have chosen to work. At this point, it is better to whisper than to shout. For the sake of this exercise, let's say that you have chosen the god-form Apollo. With strong intent, whisper, "Apollo." Inflect your voice so that the first vocalization sounds like a question, the second sounds like an affirmation, and the third sounds like joyful acceptance.

To restate:

First: Ask Apollo if He is willing to come.
Second: Accept His "yes" with a solid and clear
    acknowledgment.
Third: Greet Him with joy.

Do this three times. After the third time you should feel a warmth underneath your breastbone. Now allow yourself to "pretend" that Apollo has put part of Himself into the space underneath your breastbone. Just be with that feeling for a moment.

Now "pretend" that Apollo is talking to you. "Pretend" that He is using your mouth, your lips, and your brain with its knowledge of language to communicate with you. (I know that by this time you are feeling quite silly. But you are not silly. This is the way that the process starts, by using that wonderful magickal tool, your pretender.) Let Apollo talk. Listen with your human ears to what He is saying. It would be helpful to write it down later, in your magickal journal or in a letter to yourself.

After you feel that Apollo has talked enough, say goodbye to Him. Feel the warmth ebb away. Now, according to your preferences, you can blow out the candle or let it burn out.

Practice this "trial run" invoking for about a week. A good moon phase is from quarter moon waxing to full. Keep notes, and notice how you feel. Notice what the God-form says to you. Even though you feel funny, it's important to listen, and by listening I mean letting the God-form inside you say whatever it wants to say. Sometimes it will talk nonsense, but then, as I have said before, the Gods enjoy a good laugh. Notice if there are patterns, if themes recur. This is where your journal or the letters to yourself come in so handy: They will help you notice and keep track of the messages coming from inside your head and from the aspect of Divinity which has entered the space you have made for it. After a while, and it is short while, you will easily be able to pick which messages are from yourself and which are from the Gods. In my own case, the Gods use poetry a lot. A couple of Them speak a language I do not, but I am able to understand it while in trance.

Most importantly, the Gods never speak in absolutes, and they don't spend much time on the "poor me" issues. They ignore the possibility of failure. They *never* put you down or call you a loser or a no-good waste of time. Of course, you will sometimes feel that the negative, pessimistic view (the one that comes out of your own head) is the correct one. All I can do to reassure you is share my own experience.

For some time now, I have been in a great deal of physical pain, pain that has persisted for well over a year. My ability to do my work, typing, sewing, painting, and even brushing my teeth has been badly impaired because of a motor vehicle accident. And although I have had surgery and was (and am) doing everything I can think of to heal myself (including magick), the pain and the impairment persist.

One gray rainy day I was feeling pretty down, wondering if things would ever "go right" again. I was moaning and whining and throwing all sorts of negative energy around—and who wouldn't, in a situation like that? But worse, I was doing a head-job on myself, telling myself I was acting childishly and stupidly. After all, why should I feel sorry for myself? Just consider how bad the rest of the world has it. After all, I said to myself, I eat dinner every night.

My Big Lady Goddess has a tendency to show up at times like that, or, to be more precise, She picks me up by the scruff of my neck and plops me down in some other dimension and gives me a good talking to. In this case, I found myself sitting beside the ocean with a big black Woman sitting next to me.

"Girl, what *IS* your problem?" Her voice was warm and full of humor.

"I can't stand myself. All I do is whine and make excuses for myself, but when I try not to, the pain gets almost unendurable."

"You think you shouldn't whine?"

"No! I mean, yes! I shouldn't be feeling sorry for myself."

"Why not? If you met someone else who had your problem, would you feel sorry for them?"

"Well....yes, of course I would."

"Don't you count as a 'someone'? Shouldn't you get the same consideration you show others? Listen up, I got plans for you, and I need you to start treating 'you' nice."

And then She was gone, and I was alone with the ocean. And in my head I heard this meditation: "This is the day I have been given. I will know joy and sorrow, pain and bliss. I will meet with fools and knaves, I will be touched by evil and by virtue. I shall pass through it, my eyes always on the Star. I shall not be blinded by the Light nor the Darkness. I will look in the Shadows and the Rainbows and there I will find answers. And Her hand will hold me, Her eye will guide me."

When you feel comfortable with the "trial run" exercise, it is helpful to gather together a few friends, people you can trust. Explain to them that you are going to perform a trial run of a full-blown invocation, and that you need their assistance and tolerance.

Prepare your area, light your candles and incense, cast your circle, and call on your guardians or directional watchers. Then close your eyes.

Feel yourself anchored to the floor or ground, and then just open yourself to the energy. Don't be rushed, this process may take a few minutes. I know those few minutes can feel like hours, but in fact it takes a while for your neural net to accept the new kind of energy that will be flowing through you. You will notice your feet and hands becoming warm. That warmth will spread up your limbs and into your torso. Depending on the specific God-form with whom you are working, you will find various areas, organs, or systems glowing with heat.

Let me give you an example: if you are working with Kali, you may find not only your hands but the area behind your eyes, under your breastbone, and at the base of your spine becoming very, very warm; in fact, depending on the intent of your invocation, the feeling may become unpleasant.

On the other hand, if you are working with Apollo, you may find that your ears, shoulder blades, and hands feel as though they are full of tingling bubbles, surrounded by a clear yellow light.

Different God-forms manifest Themselves in various ways. Some God-forms use light and color; some use physical or kinetic sensations. Some use sound, while others may use taste and smell. (I have found this latter set of sensations to be most pronounced in God-forms that often or always manifest —when evoked—as animals. More on that in the section on evocation.) As you become comfortable with the process of invocation, you will find that most of the God-forms use many or all of our physical senses to indicate their presence, and each experience will be uniquely different from the others.

I know this sounds like a lot of hard work. It is. It can take days, weeks—maybe months of commitment and practice. The analogy I like to use is that you have learned how *not* to ride a bicycle. Instead, you have learned how to fall off, run into things, and get hurt. Now you are unlearning all of that learning and retraining yourself to ride a bicycle. Once you have learned how *not* to do something, it is very difficult to reawaken your repressed or crippled abilities.

Again, I want to reassure you. I know that it may seem that nothing is happening for you at first; that you are making up a lot of nonsense; that you are imagining the sensations, lights, smells, and tastes. This is where you must suspend disbelief. You need not believe in anything I have written before, nor in anything I will write from here on. But at this point you must believe in one thing—yourself. For if you do not believe in yourself, you will not have created a safe and beautiful space into which the gods may enter and abide.

I remember reading somewhere, probably in a fantasy novel, that "supposing," that is, to posit that something can and should occur, is at the very heart of magick. If you cannot "suppose" that your own power and magick will work then you will be unable to accept that Divinity will actually enjoy manifesting Itself within you.

Back to your trial-run invocation. Make sure that you ground all that energy in something—a tree, a rock, a piece of special jewelry. Take a few moments and relax. Get something to eat. Then ask for feedback. Ask for honest criticism from your fellow group members, and listen to what they say. Ask them how they felt when you performed the invocation. Do not settle for wishy-washy "OKs" or I don't knows. At this point you need specific information. You need to know the following:

1. Did they notice a difference in the energy level of the circle when you performed the invocation?

2. Did they experience any change in your voice, body stance, normal attitudes, or energy levels? In other words, was there Someone besides you inside your physical body?

3. Did what you said seem to make sense? This must be considered carefully. Given the intention and purpose of the ritual, the vocalizations of the god-form can range anywhere from cryptic to crude, with elegance and erudite understatement found somewhere in between.

Process all this information carefully. Make decisions on what you want to change and what you want to keep the same when you do the ritual "for keeps." It important that you keep in mind that up to this point you have been practicing. The motives behind the impetus to accomplish the invocation have been entirely your own. In the future that will not be the case.

11

The Primary Invoking Ritual

ΩΩ

Now you are ready to perform an honest-to-God invocation. The difference between this for-real invocation and your trial runs is that this invocation has a purpose ulterior to your own. You will therefore get different and stronger results. The other invocations had the purpose of making you comfortable with the steps; the invocation you are now going to do has another, stronger, more magickal purpose— of dedicating yourself as a priestess or priest of a specific form of Divinity. It serves the purpose of Divinity.

Collect the following items:

1. Four candles in your choice of color. These will be used to designate the four directions, or watchers. Place them in safe spots in each of the four directions.

2. A way to mark your circle or sacred space on the floor. I suggest using chalk or tape. In addition to the actual demarcation of the space, make a line about one meter (one yard) long running from east to west in the center of the space. This is where you will actually be doing the invocation.

3. A symbol of the god-form to Whom you wish to dedicate yourself. This could be anything from a statue to a book or a piece of abstract arabesque. As long as you know Who it represents, it will work.
4. Flowers, wine (or fruit juice), and a piece of whole-grain bread (leavened or unleavened).

Prepare for this ritual as you would for any other, by taking a cleansing bath with the intention of cleaning not only your body but also your emotional psyche. Clothe yourself appropriately, in clean clothing set aside for this purpose. Or if you feel more empowered by having no clothes, go sky-clad.

Do not put on any special or magickal jewelry that you might normally wear. Have the jewelry or other ornamentation set to one side of the God image or symbol.

Sweep the room with the intention of removing all negative energy from the physical area.

Discuss the purpose of the ritual with the other members of the group. Make sure that everyone understands what it is you are going to do. If anyone is uncomfortable with the intention, or doubtful that you can do it, either ask them to leave during the ritual or postpone it for the moment. Don't try to prove yourself in the face of skepticism.

What follows is a sample ritual. Please feel free to use it in its entirety, or to adapt it freely. Obviously, you do not need to use this ritual at all. Do whatever is comfortable for you.

You will be taking all the roles in this ritual unless you are certain that someone else can perform the different parts with the same intention and fervency.

Walk the circle three times, each time in a clockwise direction, starting from the northern candle.

Pointing with your right forefinger, or whatever tool you choose, walk the circle clockwise, saying: "I cast the circle in the name of the god [the name of the god you are invoking]."

You should now be back in the northern section of the circle.

Again, walk the circle in a clockwise direction, saying: "I cast the circle with the power of the Sacred Earth."

Walk the circle once more, saying: "I cast the circle by my own power."

Now step into the center of the space—but do not step over the marked line. Be careful to stay on one side of it at all times until directed to do otherwise. Raising your hands, palm upwards to shoulder level, say: "The circle is cast. The space between the worlds is made. Let all who stand here do so with a high heart and strong spirit. Let all that is not to our purpose, depart!"

Emphasize the word "depart" and bring your hands together, clapping loudly, as though ordering an unwanted guest to leave.

Now you, or someone you trust, may call the Watchers, the Directional Guardians, or the other God-forms with Whom you are comfortable working. Light the four directional candles as you do this. (Since this part of the ritual is actually evocation, I will not discuss it specifically until the second section of the book, but I suggest you do something simple and familiar. Now is not the time to introduce new and exotic elements to the ritual.)

You are still in the center of the circle, standing on one side of the line—it really doesn't matter if you stand on the south and face north, or vice versa. I find it more effective for my people to do the former rather than the latter, but that is an idiosyncrasy of my tradition.

The next thing you are going to create in this space is a cone of power. You will make it and then step into it. Read the following directions carefully and follow them closely. Failure to do so can lead to a nasty headache later.

Keeping both feet behind the line, bend down and touch the line that is in the center of the space. Focus your total attention on the middle of the circle. "See" the power starting to puddle where the line is placed. Place your hands parallel to the puddle of energy. "Feel" its heat. "Hook" your fingertips into the energy pool that is forming. (If you are able to shamanic left-shift, you will see the green-blue glow of the primal energy pool.) Raise your torso slowly, keeping your fingers connected into the pool of energy and "drag" shimmering threads of energy up from the pool as you rise.

Remember, you are not wrapping the energy around your form at this moment. You are creating a free standing energy cone in front of you, extending over the line toward you and beyond the line for about a meter.

Bringing your hands up to chest level, cross your arms so that the energy lines crisscross the space in front of your chest. Continue to raise your arms up until they are extended high above your head. "Tie" the lines of energy there, allowing them to hang in space, as it were.

Now, from the floor to the apex of the energy knot hanging in space, there is a cone of power before you into which you will step. Take a deep breath and just "be" with the flow of energy for a few moments. (Count heartbeats, it's the easiest way to measure time in a magickal circle—twenty-five heartbeats is long enough to become accustomed to the energy flow.)

Relax. Don't let your knees lock or your fists clench. Put your left foot over the line in the middle of the space and chant the following spell: (What follows is a very powerful space-shifting rhyme. I give it to you with humility and a warning: *Do not use this lightly.* Learn it by heart. Don't flub your lines!)

> *By prick of Finger*
> *And Itch of Thumb,*
> *I ken the Hag*
> *Does this way come.*
> *Now, stand I*
> *Both Out and In,*
> *As bridges meet*

Where worlds spin.
Then opens out
My smiling face
To greet the Hag
With song and grace.
For She will wear Me
Like a glove
An' She'll know Form
An' I'll know Love.

Now, step over the line.

At this point, if you have done your meditations, if you are fully aware of the god-form to whom you intend to dedicate yourself, something will happen. If you are ready, and by that I mean that you have prepared yourself to a point of sufficiency, you will experience a space-time shift. Part of you, the "watcher" part, will still be caught in the room where your body stands, but the rest of you—the real you—will go somewhere. Where? That is entirely up to the Aspect of Divinity that has chosen you. For while you may intend to dedicate yourself to, say, Isis, in truth, it is you who will be chosen. And it might be by Klotho or Coatlique or Rainbow Serpent, but by the time you step over that line, you will be ready for Whomever it is that chooses you.

I tend to go into the depths of space, finding myself perched on the edge of galaxies, watching stars being born and die. It is incredible and wonderful, but probably not at all what you will experience. Here are some experiences that have been reported by people I have trained:

Being in an intense light, a golden pink iridescent light that
   fills her, and swirling and dancing in and with that light
Finding himself in a garden, a place out of a fairy tale, being
   greeted by a shimmering person-like light form

Experiencing a place where a planet was just forming, or a
    star was becoming a nova
Drifting in a soft warm blackness

The list continues, each experience different, yet each is in one
way the same: regardless of where you find yourself, there is an
overwhelming sense of welcome and absolute love. Never forget,
Divinity wants you there.

12

Invocation of the Fourth Face

୧ଔଔ

For more than eleven years I have been dealing with the symbolism of portals: caves, gates, doors, curtains, anything that marks a change of location through a specific point of entry or exit. One October, right before Samhain, I was looking for something or Someone who seemed to be calling me. It seemed clear that this Someone or something wanted to be included in the Samhain ritual.

It was very late, or perhaps even early morning. I was working with a candle meditation and was able to get to a "space" that I had first encountered perhaps five years earlier. I was using a tape that a friend had given me, from a Pagan musical group which included some astral music that I found very conducive to meditation. I had a good steady flame on the candle and had been able to get the house quiet, with cats, children, and husband all quietly tucked in bed.

I began my ritual with a version of my personal casting and evocative calling. While I have never had any trouble raising the Directional Watchers, this night Their Aspects seemed even more clearly focused than ever before. They shimmered and danced in the energy halo located in the center of the summoning sacred space. I was elated and yet slightly frightened by the clear images which I had obtained with what seemed minimal effort. It was almost as though the way was being paved for me. I shrugged off the feelings, turned on the tape, and proceeded to summon (imagine) a door I use to enter my "otherworld" space.

However, the door that appeared was not the round-topped wooden door with brass hardware that normally appears. It was, instead, a dolmen, just one, no circle of standing stones. It was standing in the center of my field of vision, solitary and stark, arching up into a starry sky. On the "this world" side of the dolmen everything was dark and unreal as usual, but past the dolmen I could see, in very bright moonlight, a hill with low grasses blowing in a gentle breeze, several scrubby bushes near the top, and the flicker of a small fire.

As I allowed myself to "left shift" into the shamanic space, I felt myself going past the dolmen and found myself naked. Again, this was not unusual, but what was unusual was that I did not find myself taking my customary form, which is that of a large python. I continued as a human.

The wind was cool but not unpleasant. I walked up the hill, the stiff grasses pinching and poking at my feet and ankles. Since I hate being barefoot I was not too happy about this; furthermore, I could not clearly see where I was stepping. It was very real, and when I turned around, I could see, far off in the distance behind me, the room I had left and my physical body sitting in the chair where I had left it. Stretching between me and the body was the usual thin silvery thread. Since everything was normal, I turned back and began to climb the hill, disregarding my bare feet.

As I drew closer to the fire burning in a pit at the crest of the hill, the grass became softer and the light clearer. Just below the crest of the hill (it was like a foothill of a mountain range) there were several old twisted trees, bushes, and a fire. The fire was very small, the size one might use to slow-cook something. Then I noticed that there were three women seated on stones, or logs, or something, around the fire. And I knew that they were waiting for me. I wasn't frightened, just very curious as to why They had called me.

The Woman to my right was youngish with straight brown braids, very fresh in a countryish sort of way, with clear gray eyes and a dimple in her chin. She wore a light blue smocklike dress and was making a head wreath of flowers, although it was obviously late autumn.

The Woman to my left was also young but about nine months pregnant, dressed in a ruby-colored caftan that had flowers, fruit, and grasses embroidered around the hems. Her wheat-colored braids were looped up around her head and She was holding a fat contented tabby cat and had a dove perched on her shoulder.

The Woman in the center looked somewhere between sixty-five and a hundred, with a fine beautiful face, her silver hair piled up on her head. She was wrapped in a deep purple cape and was holding a long rod of silver with a shiny disk, or perhaps it was an orb, on top. When I tried to look at it too closely, I started to fall.

It was the Elder Aspect who spoke. She smiled and welcomed me, hoping that my journey had been pleasant, as though I had come a long way. She told me to sit down and warm myself, and the young one draped a gray shawllike object around me.

I noticed I was shivering, and the shawl was warm and soft. I recognized that I wanted to go to sleep immediately, so I concentrated very hard on the Crone's face. Her voice was smooth and friendly but low, and I had to listen very carefully. She called me daughter and said that She and Her Sisters were pleased with the progress that I had made and felt that I needed to move further on my path.

Then I got scared. She laughed and said I wasn't to worry about death, disasters, and losses at the moment, but that She meant I needed to explore new territories, go places I hadn't been before, and face new challenges. Somewhere inside I heard laughter, a kind of self mockery, but then I did feel a little like the crew of the Starship *Enterprise*.

She told me to relax into the shawl, which I now recognized as sleep, and to concentrate my sight on the orb on Her staff. She started to spin the staff, and as I looked into the disk I saw a hooded face bowed over, as though looking at the ground. Slowly the head raised itself until I was looking into the visage of a skull. I started to fall into the skull, and as I fell, its mouth opened and I was plummeting down into a hole of darkness, icy cold and terrifying.

Suddenly it seemed as though there was a huge mass of molten iron below me and I was falling toward it at a terrific speed. Often when we are in trance, the monsters and fears of our hidden abuse issues are brought out to confront us. I dread the sensation of falling (most people do—it is a natural startle reflex in infants), but I dread the thought of being burned even more.

The worst thing a shamanic traveler can do is clutch, or resist, even though it is the most natural and reflexive thing. I knew that if I tried to stop falling I would break apart on impact and be seared to a crisp, at least psychically. Where I got the strength from, I don't know, but I relaxed myself and gave in to the fall.

As I passed through the molten lava and fire, a piece of my skin caught and I was twirled around as all my flesh was torn from me. I remember screaming—but then I was no longer falling, I was floating.

From this point on, when I use the terms "seeing," "hearing," or others it is because I have no other terms for what I experienced. I could use "perceive," "understand," or "comprehend," but they are also related to the physical interaction of the objective and subjective. It might be clearer to say I "was" the observation, but that gets confusing. Just remember that I had no body with which to see or mind with which to know.

I soon found myself floating upward into a vast space of stars, except the stars were galaxies and the galaxies were universes. I moved rapidly through these spiraling, exploding masses of gasses, lights, and solid bits of matter. I saw things I can't begin to comprehend. One group of galaxies seemed to swallow itself and suddenly appeared behind me. Some were coming toward me, some were moving away. Some were stationary, some were "alive," while others were most certainly "dead."

As I moved through these astral phenomena, the density of the matter and energy became greater and greater. Soon I was in a densely packed universe of stars and planets, being pulled toward a shadow or absence of "thingness" at its center. I was already moving rapidly, yet I seemed to accelerate, and as I did so I began to feel incredibly small. Then I plunged into the center of the "nothingness." Suddenly I became aware of a humanlike manifestation which was outside of me and yet was within. It was the hooded figure—this time the entire body. As it turned its front toward me, I seemed to regain some of my physicalness. The awareness that It had for me was all-pervasive. Everything and everyone that I had ever been or would ever be was manifest in the awareness.

It raised Its head and I was confronted once again with the skull. As the skull regarded me, It slowly took on flesh and became the face of every woman and man that has ever existed and will ever exist. I can't explain how that could be, but It was the embodiment of everything human, self-referencing, or sapient, and very much more. It manifested itself most fully in a feminine mode because It understood, better than I ever could, why that was the most acceptable and understandable form for my present level of understanding.

Suddenly I was able to understand that this was the fourth Aspect of the Goddess, That Which lies beyond death and before birth. She was dressed in a shimmering black gown that was strewn with tiny stars and suns and moons, and when I looked at them I saw that they *were* stars and moons and suns, and many other things.

She expressed Herself as an ivory-skinned woman with long

blue-black hair and deep-blue eyes that again held the multitude of universes. She had deep full lips and clear fine coloring on high cheekbones. Her hands were slim and fine and looked incredibly capable. But the most astounding thing was the complete and unmistakable sensation of good humor that emanated from her entire vicinity. All the tolerance and compassion and level-headed judgment was there too, but the remarkable sensation of the eternal and immutable ideal of fun was like a strong perfume that completely enveloped and pervaded me.

This manifestation of Ohm/Na-Ohm was having an omnipotently good time, and *not* at my expense. There was nothing malicious or derogatory about her humor. She was in turn laughing at and with Herself and all of Creation. She took me into her awareness, almost as you or I would take a dearly loved one into our arms. As She embraced me, I was able to behold all of the people I had ever been, doing all of the things noble and vile, evil or kind, commonplace and notorious, and good and wicked committed by this entity of which I am the self-recognition. There was no judgment, no pride for good and noble actions, no shame or repugnance for the evil and foul, just a deep love and abiding respect for the entire integrity of the organism.

As far as I am able to understand or comprehend, that respect allows the self-referencing entity to foul up completely and muck around and make perfectly awful moral blunders—*and* suffer the physical and karmic consequences—without ever affecting the quality and quantity of the Divine Love. In that place of apprehension and love there was justice and mercy and a complete recognition of the uniqueness of each action without interference, approval, or disapproval. There was no punishment and no reward, only the unmovable love.

Then, behind the experience of the love came the realization of ultimate responsibility. I/It/We had created these universes, and their maintenance depended on the continuity of my/Its/Our continued process of creation. We had spoken the Word, and now it was incumbent upon us to continue to speak it, to the last syllable of utterance. It became apparent that billions and billions of sapient creatures to the billionth power and beyond, each with their hopes, dreams, and realities, were dependent on the continuous focus of the Intent of Creation. It seemed to me that She was aware of the identity of every one of those uncountable billions to the billionth power individuals and that each one mattered as much as the totality of all. In some way I understood that if She/It/We removed Our attention for even a nanosecond the entire cosmos would wink out of existence, and though that was of ultimate importance, the extinction of even one of those entities' eternal existence was of an equal importance.

Somehow the single was as paramount as the all, the one was the all, and the all was the one. And somehow the one and the all were Her/It/WE/Me. The weight of the responsibility became intense. I felt as though I were being squeezed of every thought, emotion, and reaction I had ever had or could conceive of having. I could feel myself sagging and tearing apart under the strain. I didn't want the power and I didn't want its responsibilities and consequences. The feeling became one of intense torture, of being eaten alive from the inside out. Then She "laughed"; her good humor manifested itself again and I could recognize that the maintenance of those untold billions of universes was a happy and fulfilling exercise in joy and love.

She started to dance in slow lazy spirals, and as She moved new universes spun off from the hem and sleeves of her trailing gown. Slowly She let go of me and then I was sinking down, slowly at first, through unthinkable millions of eons, and then faster, through all my superstitions and fears, reassembling my physical body, recoating myself with all the layers of karma, both positive and negative, which have enabled me to learn and grow, until I was suddenly sitting alone and naked on the moonlit hill in front of a smoldering fire. I sat there for a while and then stood up and walked down the hill. I did not look back, nor did I bother to douse the fire. I walked toward the dolmen and past it, and then I was in my room again, the tape was done, the candle was just burning out, and my entire body was cramped and tingly from having been still for so long.

I felt exhausted and yet exhilarated. I quickly released the watch towers, quit the circle, and typed the experience into my Book of Shadows.

That experience opened many new doors for me. Something fundamental inside me changed, and yet, even today, eleven years later, I could not tell you exactly what. All I know is that when I want to go there I left-shift, walk up the hill, and She is waiting.

PART III

Evocation

13

Two Actual Evocations

ℭℭ

Dark of the Moon, May 1993

The darkness settles warmly around the assembled people, comforting us and holding us. Soon it will reveal its truths. Soon it will be the stage onto which a primal and powerful manifestation of Divinity will be evoked.

There are about twenty-five of us, packed closely, knee to knee and elbow to elbow, in a small cabin tucked away in a small valley in the Catskill Mountains of New York. Outside, the early spring night is cold and sharp. The breath of the chill wind blows in through the cracks and crevices of the rudely made house.

The leader of this intense evocative ritual has told us to keep our eyes open, but I find it hard to do. I want to close my eyes and flow with the power that is being generated by this group of very magickal people. I force myself to stay with the group.

Listening carefully to the leader's words, I am carried into a place of wind and sound. His voice is clear and gentle, almost hypnotic and yet not intentionally so. He is a gifted, talented leader and knows where he will take us. At some deep level of his soul, he knows who is coming to meet us.

A shimmering light seems to fill the center of the room.

Behind me I can feel the other members of the group startle, some are even alarmed. I hear the rustling of their robes and blankets as they unconsciously try to back away from the manifestation of light in the center the circle. This is no ordinary light. Indeed, there is no light in this room. All sources of outside light have been eliminated. No, this light and its source comes from Other.

The light swirls, growing in intensity. Now there seems to be a sound emanating from it, a soft, soothing, crooning sound. I'm drawn toward the light and sound. I seem to be falling into it. Now the light has a face. It is a face I have always known. Behind me, I hear a man gasp; he sees the face also. The leader soothes the man. A wave of clear dark violet energy flows through the group as, one after another, each member sees the face, feels its power.

This evocation of the ancient Goddess of Justice has just begun. During this evocation we will call to Her in Her three aspects of Choice, Responsibility, and Judgment. Using words that we have never before heard and sounds that we have never made, Heka and her son Iacchos will join us, teach us, and empower us.

This ritual was both powerful and successful, primarily because the leader knew what he was doing. He was well prepared, and he had taken every precaution to ensure that no one, including himself, got fried or iced. Although it would violate my agreement of confidentiality to discuss the purpose of the ritual, I can say that it made a profound impact on everyone there.

Not every ritual is so successful.

Dark of the Moon, May 1997

The young man sitting to my right cries out. His hand, which had been relaxed, jerks upwards, carrying mine with it. He falls backwards, pulling the rest of us down with him. As I struggle to right myself, I can feel the thick, tearing energy of what he has called. This is not what we intended. But his nightmares, his own personal terror, have overtaken us. In a case like this I know what do. The ritual ends, then and there.

Later, shaken and aching, as I recover from a particularly nasty "ice," I ask him what happened. But he doesn't know; he had thought he was prepared, but as we talk he remembers: He had watched some old movies the night before; one of them had been *Rosemary's Baby*.

It was a good thing I couldn't move or I probably would have kicked him. He knew better than to put those kinds of images into his mind, especially right before an evocation. Now we all had to deal with the psychic residue of his perceptions of Hollywood's portrayal of the Christian Evil God. It took us all a good month to recover from his foolishness.

Movies such as *Rosemary's Baby* are what most people think of when they think of evocation—a monster manifesting itself in the middle of a pentagram marked out in blood in some basement, and the monstrous emanation of evil proves to be the undoing of the evoker until saved by some cleric. This is what many people envision, and they are wrong.

Any monsters that might manifest during an evocation are given shape and power only through the fear and misguided beliefs of the evokers. The monsters, demons, and malefic deities do not arise not from any other reality or plane of being, but are formed from unacknowledged fears and repressed incidents of pain, terror, and abuse. Divinity does not manifest as a monster, especially not as an evil God-form. Yet, unfortunately, the myth of the *powerful evoked demon*, summoned by the misguided practitioner of magick, lives on, fueled by ridiculous books and poorly written movies.

Joe, the young man who was leading the ritual, learned a hard lesson. Sometimes people have to learn the hard way. As much as we would all wish to be perfect from the beginning, it is necessary to make mistakes and deal with the consequences.

You can't learn to walk until you know how to pick yourself up from a fall.

Much of the pain that resulted from this ritual could have been avoided if Joe had paid closer attention to the three years of training he had undergone. In this kind of case, humility means paying attention to details and learning from other people's mistakes. But humility comes with experience.

Some months later, after several healing rituals and other workings by the group, I felt that Joe was once again ready to lead an evocation ritual. This time we all made sure that he watched no late-night B movies. I think he received a half dozen calls the night before the ritual, everyone making sure that his television was turned off.

That time, we had a different goal from the one when he had first attempted to lead the group. By consensus, we had decided to evoke a protective and healing Aspect of Divinity to aid us in our efforts to safeguard a threatened wetland. In detail, we had discussed who we wanted and what we would do with the energy. Joe stood in the center of the circle and began the chant: "Mother of Mysteries, That Which Abides..."

As his fine tenor voice filled the room, we all held in our minds the image of Selena, the Moon Mother.

"In-dwelling Power of Creation... Silver Arrow of Guardianship...." The image shifted from Selena to Artemis, Protectress of the wild things.

"Hold us and heal us, Provide and Protect... Give us power that we may walk in Your ways..." A sparkling green energy seemed to swirl around him, and the scent of pine needles filled the room. The power, and energy, flowed out of the shimmering light into each one of us.

One by one, we placed our request into the circle, as one would place a flower to float on the surface of a clear pond. These were the images that we had all previously agreed upon using. Each one of us waited to be led onto the next step by Joe. No one rushed ahead; no one lagged behind.

The powerful poetry of the chant continued: "... a place of growth and regeneration, a place of free nature..." Joe's voice led us onto the images of the wetlands, each member again in tune with all the others, each member forming and holding the same image, the same symbols, in our minds.

At some point it seemed that we stopped being separate individuals, that we looked upon the vision of the protected wetland with a group identity, with a powerful and cohesive evoked Aspect of Divinity holding us together. Later, each reported that we had felt a sense of acceptance and approval. This time there was no ugly energy, no threat of celluloid demons, just a compelling evocation of a powerful Aspect of Divinity.

A week later, the Environmental Protection Agency found that the wetlands in question were vital to the water table of the area and they were placed under protection.

While invocation is the calling into oneself an aspect or aspects of Divinity, evocation does something closely related and yet quite different. It creates a powerful space into which Divinity manifests in whatever form Divinity finds appropriate. The manifestation is outside of the individuals. The participants in the evocation almost always agree on what God-form manifested Itself, and their experiences of what happened at each point in the ritual have many features in common.

Many people think that invocation must be the more difficult art to practice. The calling of an Aspect of Divinity into oneself for the purposes of direct apprehension and communication seems as though it would be much more difficult than calling it into a sacred space. But I have found that that is not the case. In fact, after years of practicing both invocation and evocation, I can honestly say that evocation is much more difficult to master, for several reasons.

Invocation is primarily a solitary act, and while it is a very powerful experience it remains one that is very adaptable to the human needs of the ritual and to the person of the invoker. Once you have practiced the ritual and performed the necessary meditations and cleansing operations, invocation becomes easy and pleasurable. You do it naturally. You are the only person with whom you must agree. Your images do not need to correspond to anyone else's. The messages are usually for you and about you, and need no translation or explanation to other people. Even when the invocation has been performed within a group context, the messages usually have been for the other members of the circle, and the subjective experience of the group is all the validation that is necessary.

This is not the case with evocation. Evocation is almost always a group practice. That means that the group must, as a group, reach a consensus on the following:

1. Who or what is being called
2. The form that the invited aspect might take
3. What symbols or images will be used, from the general layout down to the smallest details
4. Why the evocation is being performed

I have found that sometimes just coming to that consensus takes up most of the time set aside for the ritual, so the ritual itself, which was meant to last several hours, is crammed into the last half hour.

Of course, this will vary from group to group. If your group has worked together often over a long period of time, say five or ten years, this agreement will come naturally. If, on the other hand, you are in the situation of most modern Pagans and find that your group seems to be forming itself anew every six months or so, you may experience difficulty coming to a working consensus. It takes time and commitment, and that is one of the reasons effective evocation is difficult. Successful evocation needs to be choreographed, much like an intricate dance.

Yet evocation is certainly worth the effort. As the members of your group become comfortable with one another and develop ways of learning to trust, anticipate each others' needs, and respect the intellectual, artistic, and emotional quirks of the fellow members, the practice of evocation will become smooth and intensely powerful.

Evocation leaves the method and the form of manifestation up to the energy of the God-form. The God-form will choose the form, shape, manner, and timing. It does not always seem to fit closely with the ritual purpose or the needs of the person or persons doing the evocation. This disconnection occurs because the participants have not considered the underlying purposes and rationale for the ritual deeply enough. In order successfully to evoke a God-form, or multiple God-forms, into a sacred space, the following issues need to be thoroughly examined and decided upon:

1. What is the purpose of the ritual? Define this in detail and be very clear as to the purpose. Do not mix purposes in rituals. Chose a God-form who is naturally aligned with that purpose. Don't choose a God-form of healing if the purpose of the ritual is financial success.

2. If the God-form is an aspect of nature, which aspect? If you need a spring shower, do not summon a summer hurricane. If you need movement, a light breeze may be more efficacious than a landslide or an earthquake.

3. Are you going to use a myth system? If so, which one? It is not a good idea to mix myth systems. If you usually work with the Greek system, don't add Egyptian or Celtic aspects. (An exception to this rule is if you are going to use multiple forms of one aspect.)

4. What did the Aspect of the Divinity you intend to evoke really mean in the context of that myth system? What does that Aspect mean to you, here and now? Is the Aspect appropriate? To answer this question, you will need the kind of knowledge of

your God-forms and their myth systems that I stressed in connection with invocation. You may want to reread pages 50 through 52.

Let's look at an example of a ritual intended to bring love into the lives of a group of people. (This premise is already fraught with peril—love is a dangerous thing to evoke, but people do it all the time.) The group has decided to evoke four forms of the Goddess of Love. They have decided that it will be most effective to use Aphrodite, Frigg, Aine, and Quetzalpetalotl. Four Goddesses and four belief systems: Greek, Norse, Erse, and Zapotec.

The members of the group read their *Bullfinch's Mythology* and *Myths of the World*, they light their candles and incense, and they *evoke!* And they get good crops, a lot of unlooked-for passion for their families, their countryside, and their cows (even if they have none), a strong hankering to form social commitments, and some brief burning ecstasy—but no love. Why not? Well, our notion of romantic love didn't exist in those four cultures. They got what they asked for; they just didn't know how to phrase the request.

To give another example, don't call on Hermes if you need someone to tell the truth. You'd do better with a Chthonic Goddess of Justice, who will probably want you to sign in blood that you won't lie when it comes your turn.

I am being deliberately facetious here, but I can't stress strongly enough that it is *vital* to know the God-form or Aspect of Divinity that you intend to evoke before you do an evocation. Don't trust for one moment the common books on mythology available at most bookstores or your neighborhood library. The myths you are likely to find in those books have most likely been bowdlerized, mistreated, mistranslated, and mutilated to conform to the prevalent belief systems of our culture.

A good place to look for mythological information is in university libraries and on the Web. If you can, go to original sources and get the best and most up-to-date translations available. Study not only the myths but the history, culture, geography, and other literature on the culture. It is not possible to understand a God-form unless you have some working knowledge of Its cultural and social context.

As I said, evocation demands a lot of work and commitment, but it is well worth the effort, and there are relatively simple ways to ease yourself into the process. The following chapters will guide you through preparing for and performing evocative rituals. Please read them carefully before you attempt a for-real evocation.

14

Evocation of the Four Elements

ഗ

This chapter contains four meditations to help you familiarize yourself with the four ancient elements, since many rituals begin with evocative warding or guarding of the sacred space with the Directional Watchers, or Elementals. As I mentioned previously, while the main cause of rituals going awry is other people, the next most common cause is the inappropriate evocation of the Directions (although misguided television and movie watching is a close third). Since most Wiccan and many Pagan rituals begin and end with these evocations, it is important to know what the directions mean and what they portend. Don't evoke the Directional Watchers casually!

The formation of group consciousness and group images takes time. In order to be effective, your group must not only do the evocations together but also the meditations, so that everyone has the same visualizations and concepts.

The following meditations are not meant to be read through swiftly as though they were some type of essay or schoolroom reading assignment. Read them carefully. Read them into a tape recorder if you have one available, or have one member of the group read them aloud. The reader should read slowly, pacing the group and giving the different areas of the meditations time to develop, with emphasis on feelings. It is important that people move through these meditations at their own pace and that they feel and come to understand the different attributes and relationships of the elements.

These meditations should take forty-five minutes to an hour and a half to complete. If you find yourself done in much less time than that, then you have probably gone too fast to get their full benefit. Again, I stress: *Don't evoke the Directional Watchers casually!*

In my tradition, water is in the East. Our reasoning is this: life begins in a watery state. The day usually begins with dew; the year begins with spring, which is a wet time, and, for us, the Mother of Waters, the Atlantic Ocean, is directly east of our homes. Therefore we start with the element of water.

In these meditations, I refer to the person doing the meditation as the aspirant, one who aspires to become one with the element, and through that conjoining to understand the power of the Direction and the Watcher.

There are altars in these meditations, for I find that such a focus is often very helpful and serves as a way to demarcate the space and time from ordinary relaxation and dream time.

Meditation of Water

In this meditation the aspirant becomes one with the element of Water in order to know it in all of its phases and its emotions. The area in which the person or persons is working should be cool but not uncomfortably so.

For your own comfort, don't do these meditations in robes or vestments. If possible, you should wear flowing loose clothing so that movement is not impeded. Have enough pillows and bolsters so you can lie propped on the floor comfortably.

The altar is set with the two sacred candles lit, a symbol of Water between them, and before the altar a large bowl of clear water.

Stand in front of the altar and take a series of three deep breaths, hold each for a count of three, and release each one with a series of three blows. A feeling of moist coolness should flow through your limbs. Repeat the breathing exercise nine times, in three groups.

In the first group of breaths see the color of the air entering your body as a silver misty blue and the air leaving as a rust orange. In the second group of breaths the color of the incoming breath is a clear pond blue and the outgoing breath is a muddy brown. In the last group the inhaled breath is a deep-sea-green blue and the exhaled is a tarry black.

Take the basin or bowl of water and place it on the floor or ground in front of you. Put your hands into the basin, holding your hands in the water, and concentrate on the physical feeling of the water. Then evoke the powers of Water with the following words. (Don't worry that they seem uncomfortable or strange. These elementals know when they are being called upon with respect. It is okay to read this aloud the first several times you do this meditation):

Ladies and Spirits of Water, and You,
Most Ancient and Beloved Ybbgillia,
I call upon You to come to me and immerse me in the depths
  of Your wisdom and power.
Teach me to know you with all the strength of my heart and
  spirit.
Let me drink deeply of your knowledge.
Eldest Mother, Tiamat, from whom the world was made, Show
  me your depths and teach me your laws.
Lovely Cynthia, Moon Maiden, You who pulls upon the tides
  and the seasons,
I ask that You keep me in safety while I abide within Your
  watery realms, that I do not drown in waters too deep or
  rough.

> Lady Elaine, discover to me the strengths and the failings of
> the Lake, that I may learn to navigate its waves and master
> its mysteries.
> For it is I, [your name], your son/daughter and brother/sister
> who claims as his/her inheritance this wisdom and
> knowledge.

Now lie on your back, knees and head propped so your back
does not become uncomfortable and you can gaze into the basin.
Check your abdomen and chest carefully to see if there is any
residue of tension; if there is, repeat the breathing exercises.

See yourself floating in a clear blue pool of light. As you float
you slowly become aware that the pool of light is beginning to
flow and ripple around you, and you are being rocked back and
forth, gently at first, but after a while more vigorously.

Let the waters of the pool wash over you and the current draw
you down into the depths. Relax! Breathe normally. After all,
you are in the element of love and protection and nothing will
hurt you here.

Now imagine that the pool is connected to the ocean, and the
current has pulled you out to the sea. Flow with it, rock on the
waves.

Soon you are tossed onto the surface of this great sea. You look
around, but there is no land in sight. The waves are turning into
large breakers and you feel the exhilaration of the pounding surf
within your body. The surf is pounding in the rhythm of your
heartbeat. You can hear the surf crashing on a distant shore.
Slowly, the tide carries you toward that shore.

A bank of dark clouds rolls in and the water of the heavens joins
the water of the sea. You are washed closer to land, and as you near
the beach the wind scoops you up and you are carried upward,
into the roiling clouds. You are borne inland, high in the air over a
vast range of craggy mountains, where you feel your body
becoming sharp intricate ice crystals and falling silently down to
the slopes of the mountains. Really feel the cold and solidness of

that form of water. Be the winter storm that rushes up into the mountains, filling the valleys with silent snow.

The wind carries you up and over the mountains, and now, on the other side, as you drop down closer to the earth, you become rain. Below, you notice a vast fire, the trees nothing but smoking sticks, the earth black and hot behind the roaring flames. You feel the appeal of the scorched earth. You feel the release of yourself, the relaxation of all tension as you dissolve into the cooling life-bringing rain. As you wash the earth clean, you carry the debris and nutrients released by the fire into a channel where you become a steady creek, a rapid brook, and then, surging with more and more of your power, a mighty river as you rush down through the floodplain.

You now become a raging ugly flood. You break over the banks, drowning all that lies before you, depositing the rich burden of river silt across the land.

You smash and rage, uprooting trees and tearing down cities and farms. Then you become the hopeless rage and anger of the people on the high places who stare down at you in bitter reproach. You are the black unrelenting hatred of the mother whose child has died and you feel the sickness of the mob as it hangs the man whose carelessness allowed the dam to break. Then you become peaceful again, flowing back into your channels and smoothly out to the sea.

Now, lie quietly and imagine yourself as a vast field of silent snow. You feel the incredible potential of the earth below you. Feeling the heat of the sun, you begin to melt, soaking into the dry earth and flowing away into the rivers and streams. As you sink into the earth, you awaken all the forces of life: the seeds, roots, insects, and worms. You roust the fish and frogs from their winter lethargy and call to the animals in their holes. You feel the swelling of the buds on the trees as the sap rises in elation at the spring.

You become not only Water, but joy and love. You throb in the loins of the lovers lying in the sweet grass under the full moon of

Beltaine. You stir the hearts of the people with compassion at the sight of the newborn, and you are now the laughter in the hearts of children.

Allow that laughter to become the bubbling of a clear spring of water, sparkling happily up from the depths of an underground river, and as you bubble and splash people come and scoop you up in buckets. Imagine yourself being poured into cups and giving life to the drinkers. See the infant being washed of its birth-blood in your warm cleansing fluid. You clean the dirt from the hands of the workers and the soil from their clothing. You are poured out for the thirsty plants and animals. Finally, you wash the corpse before burial and sting the eyes of the mourners as a bitter gray rain.

You now become the empty wailing of grief and desolation that plunges into the black maw of despair and finally surfaces once more on the calm tide of acceptance and consolation.

Now you condense yourself into a tiny drop of water, a prismatic colored orb containing all the life force of Water, with all of its fluid emotions. Take the mental image of the drop of water and place it in the chakra under your lower left rib cage, where it will reside in the center of a lovely flower. Place your hands back in the bowl of water and thank the Powers of Water:

Ladies and Spirits of Water, I give you my thanks and my honor.
Great Tiamat, I honor and worship You.
Lady Elaine, I thank You.
I have been safely through your realms
Of sea and storm, river and stream,
Of love and hatred, despair and consolation.
Cynthia, You have cradled my birth upon your waves, and
  have swept me with death upon your flood, bringing me
  full cycle in your healing rains. All that You are, now I am.
  For I am, [your name], your son/daughter and brother/
  sister, an undine of water.

Now repeat the breathing exercises that began this meditation, but as you blow out the blue light held within you, see it replaced by a rosy opal flecked with flashes of silver and sapphire. Place the gem directly into the flower beneath your breastbone. Since opals must be kept in water, you should imagine the drop of water enveloping the gem.

This ends the Meditation of Water.

Now consider some of the god-forms associated with Water and the east. Ybbgillia is an ancient Sumerian mermaid, perhaps the oldest known mermaid form. She is a love Goddess, the middle daughter of Tiamat (Old Mother).

Aphrodite is another God-form associated with water. She is born of the waves, or the foam of the waves. In later myths she is formed of the semen that was spilt from Kronos' testicles when they were cut from His body and flung into Ocean.

Yemaja, the western African Goddess of Love and fertility, is also associated with water.

Water is seen as a feminine element, but many masculine God-forms are associated with the more violent aspects of it. Yahweh was sometimes seen as a two-tailed sea serpent and a God of Thunder. Poseidon is the God of Oceans but not necessarily of water. And for all the worship of Au-set and Osiris, Aten and Horus, the God at the very heart of the Egyptian civilization is the Nile.

Since human life cannot exist without water, it is understandable that as an elemental it is primary to our physical and magickal existence. But it is not always sweetness and love. It contains within itself all emotions, from doting adoration to implacable hatred, and those far-ranging emotions must not be ignored if a ritual evocation is to be done. If you have angry people in your ritual space, then the emotions of anger, fear, and hatred will come as surely as love and trust when water is evoked.

Allow yourself and your group a rest of several days between the Meditation of Water and the Meditation of Fire.

Meditation of Fire

In this meditation you take on the attributes of Fire so that you may fully understand, communicate, and control the ethereal element of fire and the powers of the spirit, will, intuition, and courage.

The room should be comfortably warm but not stuffy. Again, you should be dressed in comfortable nonrestrictive clothing. The altar should have only the two sacred candles lit, with a symbol of Fire between them. A drawing of a flame can work, but it is preferable to do some imaginative thinking and come up with your own way of symbolizing the concepts of courage, intuition, will, and spirit. Give this some thought, because fire is an element that we tend to neglect.

Place a sturdy fat candle, one that has a large flame, in front of but not blocking the symbol.

Have a chair for each person performing the meditation. Arrange them so everyone has a clear view of the candle. Seat yourself comfortably with your spine straight and chin level. Breathing in deeply through your nose, hold for a count of seven, release slowly through the mouth to a count of seven. On the first breath, "see" all the air rushing into your body as warm orange and the air being expelled as dirty olive gray. On the second breath, again see the color but with a greater intensity, and also feel a pleasant degree of heat in the lower limbs. Increase the intensity of color and heat throughout your entire body with each breath but not to the point of discomfort.

As you gaze intently into the flame, say the following words to evoke the powers of Fire:

Lords and Spirits of Fire, and You, my Prince Tezcatlipoca,
Come to me for I approach You, Asking that You teach me of
  Your nature and Your power.
Let me become as one with You.
Let me be a flame of courage,

A blazing hearth where intuition and will can reside
And a catalyst for transformation.
Goddess Hestia, who keeps the sacred flames burning, protect
*   me from all danger on this my quest for knowledge.*
Much maligned Loki, show me the tricks and ruses of the
*   flames.*
Wayland Smith, instruct me in the practical uses of this energy
*   of work.*
Pan, you who spoke from the primordial torch, speak to me
*   now in words that my mind and spirit can understand.*
It is I, [your name], your beloved sister/brother and daughter/
*   son, who claims as her/his rightful inheritance the*
*   knowledge and powers of Fire.*

Now mentally cleanse the area in which you are working, seeing everything consumed by an intense flame until the area is clear of any outside forces or connections. Then cleanse yourself, starting with your feet and progressing to the crown of your head, until you see yourself as a clear transparent flickering flame, burning without being consumed.

Begin the meditation by imagining a black void. Just allow yourself to float in the void for several minutes. Then see a point of flame moving rapidly toward you from far away. Feel its longing, its desire for union, as it meets you and both you and it explode in a tremendous flare.

Now allow yourself to see a barren planet with flames spouting out of crevices and mountains being heaved up with great red gouts of fire and lava. You are the fire; you are the white flame burning across the black skies, rocks, and stones melting and coalescing in front of your creative fury. At this point feel the fires of creation, see the gases forming huge clouds and finally the rains pouring out of a sky now filled with roiling clouds.

Now imagine yourself as a hearth fire. Feel the kindly nurturing warmth you are giving out. See the children and the adults lean toward you for warmth. Allow yourself to be the warmth that comforts their bodies, the wholesome food being prepared with your heat. Hear the crackle and hiss of your flames as you convert the wood and/or coal into energy. Throughout your body, feel the change from static energy within the fuel to moving energy. See yourself escaping up the chimney and dissipating into the cool air.

Now imagine a great forest, high trees with a mass of impenetrable thorns and decaying undergrowth. Feel the dry autumn air and the heaviness of the approaching storm. Become the flash of lightning that streaks down from the skies and hits the old dead pine. Feel the heat of the blaze as it spreads rapidly, setting all around it on fire also. Soon you are a great conflagration, swept by wild winds generated by your own heat, feeding on all the dead and dry vegetation, eating everything in your path.

Everything that can run flees in front of you until you are finally stopped by a broad river. Soon all that can be burned is charred ashes. Your last flames flicker bravely as a soft rain begins to fall.

You now draw yourself together into a tiny but intense piece of energy. Project yourself into the candle in the middle of the altar and see yourself providing light for scholars, scientists, and doctors—light for learning, light for change. Feel the process of change, including the courage to change.

Expand yourself into the pit of a blast furnace, feeling all the power of manual labor and the effort of work. Finally you become the flame of the rocket engines as a spacecraft lifts away from the planet's surface and you are once again a point of flame floating in a vast black void.

Now mentally form all the energy you have just experienced into a glowing red-orange globe in the palms of your hands. Acknowledge that you and it are the one and same. The globe becomes a clear blood red ruby which you place directly just above your pubic bone.

The aspirant now thanks and releases the powers of Fire:

I give you, O Lords and Spirits of Fire, my thanks and my
    honor. I have felt your power and heard your message.
Great Mother Hestia, I give you thanks that I have stood safely
    amid the flames and have not been seared by them.
Loki, you have shown me the destruction of your blaze, but I
    saw also the cleansing and new life which you brought to
    the land.
Wayland, you have placed before me the works and uses of
    Fire's energies.
Goddess, from the stars You brought me forth and to the stars
    You shall return me. My honor and thanks, for I am [your
    name], *your daughter/son and sister/brother, a crystal*
    salamander who dances in the eternal fire of Your Love.

Now repeat the sevenfold breath, this time replacing the fiery
colors with a clear white light flecked with flashes of gold and
ruby and the warmth with a sense of pleasing coolness.

Here ends the Meditation of Fire.

As you work with the element of Fire, you will find yourself
leaving the strictly physical part of Fire and moving into the
aspects of courage and intuition. You will find that the Gods of
prophecy, such as Tezcatlipoca and Loki, are ardent keepers of
the flame, as is ancient Pan, the Spark of Desire for Whom the
World Was Created. Follow these God-forms into the Burning
Spire of the World Tree and see what They may teach you.

Again, allow a space of a few days to absorb what you have
learned before you move on to the Meditation of Air.

Meditation of Air

In this meditation you will seek to experience, assimilate, and
command the element of Air, becoming one with it and
mastering its power of intelligence and mind.

It is best to do this meditation when there is a window open to admit a gentle breeze, and again when the sounds of strong winds can be heard. Wind chimes that can be clearly heard can be an asset to this meditation. A tape with the sounds of wind blowing, in all of its many variations, is invaluable.

The altar is lit with two white candles, a symbol of Air, and a fresh incense like sandalwood. You should be dressed in loose comfortable clothing and the room should be dimly lit. Soft music may help, but play it very low.

Begin the meditation by sitting comfortably in a chair, gazing into the smoke of the incense. Take five deep breaths in through your nose and release them through your mouth. Imagine the breath going in as a clear clean yellow and exiting as a foul purple-green. With each breath, your body should fill with the clear yellow light and become lighter and lighter. Your breathing should continue and intensify as you imagine yourself starting to float up into the air and dissolving onto the breeze (or storm, as the case may be).

You now invoke the powers of Air:

Lords and Ladies of Air, and you my Lord TaHuti,
I call upon you to teach me the way of the winds and
*   tempests.*
Great Apollo, lift me upon your mighty breezes that I may
*   know from where and to whence the winds do blow.*
Most ancient Isis, place me within the life-engendering power
*   of first breath and allow me to go into the place beyond*
*   forever as I give forth my final gasp.*
Guide me, Sophia, Lady of the Western Sunset, that I may
*   know Your realm in all of its complexities, and give me your*
*   wisdom and clear knowledge.*
For it is I, [your name], Your beloved son/daughter and
*   brother/sister who calls upon You, in the many names of*
*   Goddess, who claims this knowledge as his/her rightful*
*   inheritance.*

You see yourself drifting over the sea, lightly lifting the water into waves, pulling water up into yourself and then sweeping in over the land and blowing strongly through the trees and tall grasses. You hear the sounds of your passing as you rustle the leaves and rattle the dry grass.

Feel yourself blowing harder and harder until you are shrieking through the mountain passes and roaring across the desert carrying tons of sand before you. Allow yourself to bury the foolish traveler who did not listen to the warnings of the wise elders. Allow yourself to lay bare the ancient knowledge so long hidden beneath the sands of time. Blow hard!

Now you quiet and become a warm gentle breeze again, carrying the scent of the newly blooming fruit trees into the villages and towns. Tangle yourself in the hair of the maidens and blow the clothing on the line dry. Fill the nostrils of the infant at birth, and as the babe breathes you in, see her soul entering her tiny body. You are filled with the awe of the life that you bring to every living thing. You see yourself carrying golden energy into the grasses, trees, flowers, and into every type of living creature, including microscopic ones.

Now change the image to that of sooty gray smoke, carrying all sorts of germs and pestilence. You are the toxic gases spewed out by volcanoes and factory stacks; you are the smelly vapor from a fetid swamp. You feel the caustic burning with each breath.

Allow yourself to be the intelligence and reason that finds ways to remedy the damage, that invents methods of production that are not polluting, that gains knowledge of conservation and ecological balance. Become that wisdom, holding it securely within you. You then become the chill blast of Arctic air that rips the leaves from the trees and freezes the bog so that the air is clean and hard. Allow yourself to howl among the bare branches and soar high toward the frozen stars. Then softly sink down again to rest, gently caressing the waves of the ocean.

As you rest over the ocean you become aware of the light which passes through you You see clearly all the different colors and feel the pulsating energy of the different wave lengths. You become the red light and are made hot by passion and raw life energy, then you are a clear relaxed orange, tingling with attraction and positive experience. The orange becomes the clear yellow of health and mental alertness, the pure gold of the sun. From this comes a clear deep emerald green, the color of fertility and prosperity, which gradually becomes the sparkling azure blue of intelligence and intuition. The blue deepens, like a January evening, into a pure violet of spiritual wisdom which rapidly turns into the royal purple of power. Now you are the rainbow with all the colors swirling around and through you, dissolving into a blaze of dazzling white light.

Through the white light you are lifted upward and become aware of the vibrations of matter which condense into clearly comprehended sounds: the soft sighing of lovers in each others' arms, the scream of a woman in labor, the wail of the newborn as it greets its new body and life. The laughter of children and the angry shouts of fighting youths. The busy clatter of machinery and the soft lowing of peaceful animals. The snap of the fire and the purr of the cat. The chant of the priestess and the angry roar of the mob. The keening of the bereft and the silence of death. You become all of these.

Then you feel yourself becoming one with the cutting edge of a logically sound argument, and the fuzzy warmth of an intuition. You experience the sickening jolt of unexpected clairvoyance. Finally you become the serene calm space of wisdom which can acknowledge its own finiteness and illogicality.

Now you will experience, directly in front of you, a pillar of light and sound, carved with every piece of wisdom and knowledge that has ever existed and will ever exist. Look at it closely. Notice the handholds, the places for foot and finger and seeking mind. You start to climb, ascending the pillar, and soon you have the sensation of being swept up as though into a vacuum. At the top of the pillar you see a shining doorway with "Truth" inscribed over the arch. You walk through it and immediately find yourself falling into a pit of chaotic darkness. You realize that the truth is both the light and the dark, the order and the chaos, the logic and the intuition. You understand that there is no One Truth.

At last you become a wind of creation, flaring millions of miles out from the surface of a star, and in the depths of your being you carry the seeds of another universe. Allow yourself to experience that reality for a few moments, to be the Cause and the Question.

Now condense all of the energy of this flaring wind into a serene deep blue sapphire. As you slowly sink back into your body (did you just now notice that you were out of it?), place the gleaming gem between and slightly above your eyes. Now release the powers of Air:

> *Lords and Ladies of Air, I thank you for guiding me and*
> *   filling me with your knowledge and reason.*
> *I have ridden upon your winds and have felt the force of your*
> *   hurricanes.*
> *Let me always remember the lessons I have learned at your*
> *   hands. For I am your beloved son/daughter and brother/*
> *   sister, [your name], a sylph of the air.*

Rest quietly for several minutes and then write down any intuition or revelation which may have occurred to you. Blow out the candles.

This ends the Meditation of Air.

Wisdom is not the same as learning, and knowledge is not the same as logic. We are a people encumbered by words, and while those words are very useful in helping us communicate, often internal communication does not come in the form of words. True wisdom lies in listening to all the messages that come our way, whether or not they are carried in word packages.

Gods of Wisdom are many. I can't think of a culture that has not honored wisdom and knowledge. But the way an ancient culture imagined knowledge, learning, and wisdom may be very different from the way a present-day culture thinks of them. Be clear about what you want to know when you evoke Gods of Wisdom and Knowledge. You may not like what you learn.

For some reason it is best to work with the preceding three meditations several times each before going on to the Meditation of Earth. It may have something to do with the fact that Earth is slow and doesn't like to be hurried.

Meditation of Earth

This may be the most difficult of the meditations of the four classical elements, for it is heavy, slow, and tightly packed, like earth itself. It is good to do this meditation when you can be in direct contact with the ground, but since that is rarely feasible, instead try holding a midsized rock during the entire meditation and attempt to follow the vibrations that may emanate from the rock.

During this meditation you will seek to confront and overcome the obstacles of the rigidity and solidity of Earth and discover the empty spaces and the glittering halls of wonder that are the basis of all that is observable and touchable. It helps to remember that we are able to perceive a form or an object because of the spaces of the so-called no-thingness around it.

The room should be warm and your clothing should be snug yet comfortable. A feeling of closeness, yet not one of constriction, is wanted.

The altar is set with two white candles, a symbol for Earth (I often use a clod of rich soil with several rock crystals embedded in it), and warm musky incense.

Now evoke the powers of Earth:

Powers of Earth,
Ladies and Lords of the Mountain Halls,

Bhan a'Sidhe, Master Red Hat,
And You, my Queen Goruda,
I call upon you to aid me in this quest.
Guard me, Hephaestus and Persephone. Let me not be lost in
your mazes and vaulted passages. Teach me of matter and of
time, that I may know my finite mortality and my infinite
existence.
For I am your beloved sister/brother and daughter/son, [your
name], *and I claim this knowledge as my rightful*
inheritance.

Lie down in a comfortable fetal position and place your rock
near your heart. Take a series of eight slow breaths and pause,
repeating this three times.

Each breath goes in a pure royal purple, and as you exhale the
air comes out a dirty grayish yellow. With each breath you feel
yourself becoming heavier and heavier, being filled with an
awesome power as you sink into the bowels of the earth. Allow
yourself to sink lower and lower and feel the warmth of the core
of the earth coming toward you. You feel the pressure of the
millions of tons of rock all around you, and yet you are heavier
and more solid than all of it.

Take several minutes to sink into the earth, until at last you
find yourself at the center of all matter, white hot and
tumultuous with radioactive energy. The pressure of the matter
becomes stronger and stronger, and you feel yourself pushing
and pushing, like a woman in labor. Then the continental plates
give way and you come boiling upward until you erupt from the
womb of the volcano in a fiery stream of lava and ash arching
across the sky.

You have become a molten river, and find yourself pouring
down the side of the mountain, causing the ground to scream
and moan beneath your heat and weight. Really allow yourself
to feel, to intimately experience the weight. Slowly you cool and

come to a final hissing steam bath as you plunge into the sea. Now you can feel the wind rubbing against you and the cold and heat of the passing years breaking you apart. The tiny roots of mosses and lichens and then trees and flowers reach into you for foundation and sustenance.

Give yourself several minutes to feel the soft carpeting of the fallen leaves and petals and the rich smell of death as they break down and decay. Then open yourself, allowing your weighty massive self to become the resting place of insects, amphibians, reptiles, mammals, and birds, feeling the warmth of their living bodies and the cold heaviness of their dead carcasses. Allow yourself to be that which allows them to turn full cycle.

The seeds fall and nestle into you, and you cradle them as the cold snow blankets you. Let the feeling of deep coldness permeate you. Feel yourself slowing down, the inertia of the physical universe dragging at you. Slowly you grind to a halt.

Take your time with this resting phase. At length you will feel a tiny throbbing of energy at the base of your spine. Allow it to grow. As it grows it warms you, and you can feel the pulsing of life in the seeds and the restless and relentless pushing as they struggle up to greet the air. You can feel the warmth of the rain as it soaks into you, making you heavy and drowsy, sensual and sexual.

Desire for life can be imagined as a warm rosy glow which starts in your genitals and spreads rapidly throughout your torso and limbs. The animals dig into you for burrows and dens and you make them welcome. Then you feel the step of humankind, the cut of the plow, and the careful placing of the precious seed grain.

You open yourself to the ritual of the Grain Goddess, pouring a rich red-gold energy up into the plants (a feeling much like climax) and you rejoice in how they thrive and the cycle continues.

Rest with that feeling a moment. In fact, let it revolve in several cycles. Then allow yourself to sink once more and become a dark empty space, a void within the fold of stone. The mountains creak and whine around and above you, and as the mountains shift restlessly, like huge children dancing from foot to foot, the entrance to your space breaks open and you are filled with blazing brilliance as the sunlight strikes your glittering crystals and flashing gems. Men come and call you holy and take the gems from your flesh. Become the gems—the clear diamond, the red ruby and yellow topaz, the green emerald and blue sapphire and purple amethyst.

You become the heavy yellow-gold and cool white-silver, which men fashion into settings for the jewels. Allow yourself to experience the heaviness and the close finiteness of yourself. You feel treasured and precious.

Now shift to another image: imagine yourself as heavy red iron ore being melted and purified in a blast furnace and poured out hard and gray. You are pounded and heated and pounded again until you have become both the plow that will cut the body from which you came and a sword that will cut the body of the cutter. Stay with this image for a while. Consider what it means to be both a sword and a plow, and the metal from which they are made.

As you experience yourself as the metal of sword and plow, you are also the rust of time that eats them away, returning them to their original natures. For time is an essential aspect of the Element of Earth.

To experience time, you must first place yourself outside of it. Try to view time as a opalescent ameba with a cloudy perimeter that at any given point may be extending itself or retracting into itself. The touch of the time-ameba can at once constrain and hold constant things that have happened. It can also touch the future possibilities and probabilities (sort of like the pilot wave in quantum physics) and when it pulls back into the "present" brings information about the possible and probable futures with it. Thus, with that information the future helps form the past and present.

Watch the Ameba. Dance with the Ameba. Allow yourself to

see it slowly vanish like mist into a velvety nothingness in which numberless motes of life energy are floating.

At this point you are able to sense yourself as the protector, but not the director, of these "souls." With care, and not pushing yourself into something that you feel incapable of doing, call the life energies toward yourself. You and they will coalesce in a whirling spiral of light which slowly spins faster and faster until you can feel the particles of energy solidifying into stars and planets. Now you must abruptly let the sensations of the meditation go, almost snapping free, so that the work of your creation can progress according to the Universe's infinite laws.

As you snap free you will feel heavier and slower and will find it helpful to bring your attention back to your rock, focusing on it to reconnect you with the earth.

Repeat the breathing exercise, but at the end of it turn the royal purple light into a clear transparent brilliancy. Now turn the clear light into a large multifaceted diamond full of green and violet lights, and place it at the base of your throat, in the notch of your collarbone.

Rest quietly for a few minutes, and then eat and drink some prepared foods. Only when that is done should you thank and release the powers of Earth, as follows:

Ladies and Lords of the Earth, I thank you for your guidance.
Ancient and august Persephone and Hephaestus, You have led
*   me truly through Your passages of knowledge and wisdom. I*
*   have experienced both my impermanence and my eternity.*
Great Dia, Mother of Earth, I give You my worship.
Rhea Kronos, You have allowed me to glimpse Your riddle of
*   time. I bow before Your majesty and power.*
For I am your beloved daughter/son and sister/brother, [your
    name], *a child of Time and Earth, and as I will it, so shall*
*   it be.*

The Meditation of Earth is now ended.

After each meditation you will find it useful to write any thoughts, questions, and revelations in your journal, or if you have one, your Book of Shadows.

Gods and Goddesses of Earth are many. Some are Grain goddesses such as Demeter; others are Chthonic Goddesses such as Heka (Heka-te is not a Goddess; she is a human priestess whose name means "old one of Heka"), or the Gods of the Afterlife, such as Aides (Hades). Notice that they are not the Gods of Death: Thanatos is a God of Air, not of Earth.

Again, use a great deal of care when evoking the God-forms of Earth; They are heavier and mightier than you might expect.

I practice each of the meditations of the elements once a month. I have been doing so for almost fifteen years and still learn something new each time.

15

Evocation of Divination

ΩΩ

By now I am certain that you have the concept of evocation well in hand. The core idea is subjectively to know and understand the cultural and physical aspects of the god-form you intend to evoke and then allow it to fill the space you have made in whatever manner it chooses. Secondary to that, but almost as important, is not to have bizarre images in your mind, and if they are there, to clean them out.

I will close this section on evocation with an actual evocative ritual that my group and I use.

Evocation of Divination

This ritual is best done at a full (mother) moon, since it is done to attain true dreams, clear foresight, and prophecy. It is an evocation of those god-forms which control the process of divination. The God-forms used in this ritual come from the Greek pantheon. They are:

Pythia: The Snake Goddess of Delphi. She is an Earth Element. Her home is the Omphalos, the earth navel.

Apollo: Before He was a Sun God He was a God of Divination, truth, and prophecy, as well as healing and wisdom. He is a Fire Element. He superseded Pythia at Delphi, but She remained the voice of the oracle that Apollo used at Delphi.

Métis: The Goddess of Memory. She is a Water Element.

Hermes: The God of Trickery, Illusion, and Lies. He is the shadow on which Apollo's light can be clearly seen, and no one knows the difference between truth and deception as well as Hermes. Hermes is an Air/Wind Element.

Out of relatively small pieces of paper, make brightly colored symbols of each of the four God-forms or elements. It is best to keep these paper symbols both simple and bold, and thus more easily remembered. For example, Water could be a blue-green drop, Fire a red-yellow flame, Air a yellow-silver swirl, and Earth a purple-green square. Work with the images until you and the others in your group can instantly bring them up when the appropriate element is called.

Now add a symbol that denotes the God-form. A snake in a square would be appropriate for Pythia, while an open eye in the middle of a flame could indicate Apollo. A door in the drop of water could be Métis, and a teeter-totter set to balance in the swirl of Air is appropriate for Hermes. Again, work with the images.

Before you attempt the ritual, agree on the order in which the God-form images will be considered and the length of time each image will be held in consciousness. Since it is hard to time mental actions, use a specific number of heartbeats. Fifteen is usually sufficient.

Set up an altar at the western end of your working space. Use four candles, two white and two black. Incense, such as frankincense, should be ceremonial. A black mirror or a gazing crystal should be in front of the candles and the incense burner. It should be easy to reach.

Select a person to cast the circle and another to evoke the watchers. One person will evoke the female God-forms and another the male God-forms. (Of course, it is possible that one person alone can perform this ritual. It is simply easier if there are several people—and there is more power from the effect of group consciousness.)

The caster starts in the north and walks around the space clockwise (deosil), saying:

"I cast this circle in the name of Truth, that we may know it when we find it.

"I cast this circle in the name of Balance, that we may not stumble in the darkness nor be blinded by the glare of pure light.

"I cast this circle in the name of Foretelling, that we may use the power to chart our course through time and space.

"Thus I have cast this circle."

The caster rejoins the other members of the group and says: "The circle is cast, the space between the worlds is made. Let all who stand herein do so of their own free will, with a high heart and steady spirit. Let all that is not to our purpose—depart!"

The person chosen to evoke the watchers goes to the eastern sector of the circle. Using whatever tool that is deemed appropriate (including the human finger) the caller points to the east while he says:

> *From Your Eastern Waters*
> *And the Memories of Eternal Springtime,*
> *From the Break of Day,*
> *I ask that you come to us, Mother of All Emotions.*
> *Come, flow through us, that we may know You.*
> *Come, stand here with us,*
> *Guard and Guide us.*
> *We bid You Welcome."*

All of the other members of the group should then respond, "We bid You welcome."

The caller goes to the southern sector, and using the appropriate tool, points to the south and says:

> *From Your Southern Fires,*
> *From the blazing Sun of Summer*
> *From the heat of Midday,*
> *I ask that you come to us, Bright God of Wisdom,*
> *Come, burn within us, that we may know You.*
> *Come, stand here with us,*
> *Guard and guide us.*
> *We bid You welcome.*

All of the other members of the group should respond, "We bid You welcome."

The caller goes to western sector and repeats his actions, saying:

> *From the Western Winds,*
> *From the changing notes of Autumn,*
> *With all the colors of the Evening Sky,*
> *I ask that you come to us, Lord of Illusion,*
> *Come, move within us, that we may know You.*
> *Come, stand here with us,*
> *Guard and guide us.*
> *We bid You welcome.*

Again, all of the other members of the group should respond, "We bid You welcome."

Finally, the caller goes to the northern sector and evokes Pythia: (She is heavy and slow but moves with a vast power; be sure to give her plenty of time to enter.)

> *From the Northern Sacred Stones,*
> *From the solid space of Winter,*
> *From the center of All-being,*

From the bone and sinew of Reality,
I ask that You come to us, rooting Yourself within
*   us, O sacred Pythia, Goddess of Prophecy, that*
*   we may know You.*
Come, stand here with us,
Guard and guide us.
*   We bid You welcome.*

The caller takes his place in the group and says: "We stand in the presence of our Sacred Watchers. Let all that we do and say be pleasing in Their sight."

The person who has been designated to evoke the Female God-forms steps into the middle of the space. Touching the floor, then her heart area, and then her forehead, she raises her arms in the air and says: "Ancient and Potent, Far-Seeking, Truth-Telling, enter this space so that we, your children, your brothers and sisters, may see clearly." She lights the black candles.

The person who has been designated to evoke the male God-forms performs the same actions, saying: "Ancient and Potent, Far-Seeking, Truth-Telling, enter this space so that we, your children, your sisters and brothers, may see clearly." He lights the white candles.

As the God-forms are evoked, everyone in the sacred space must consciously recall the images that were made, in the order that the group agreed upon, and hold these images for the agreed-upon length of time.

The person who cast the circle now steps to the altar and takes the scrying mirror or crystal and does a divination for the person who called the elements. Keep the time of scrying brief; remember that the others are holding the power in place. Also, a time limit will cause you to rely more deeply on intuition and less on what might be socially appropriate. Don't second-guess yourself. Trust to the God-forms that what you say is accurate.

The caller then scrys for the person who evoked the female

God-forms, she scrys for the next person, and so it goes until the last person for whom the scrying is done is the circle caster. (Don't attempt to scry for yourself. Therein lies self-deception!)

For the space of about a hundred heartbeats, let everyone sit with their divination. Then the person who evoked the male God-forms stands, and raising his hands in the air, slowly lets them drop to his side, saying: "Ancient and Beloved, we thank You for these gifts. I bid You farewell."

The rest of the group responds, "Farewell."

The person who evoked the female God-forms stands, raises her hands in the air, and slowly allows them to drop to her side, saying: "Ancient and Beloved, we thank you for these gifts. I bid You farewell."

The rest of the group responds, "Farewell."

The person who called the Elementals now takes the paper symbols and burns them in the appropriate candles, the female in the black candles and the male in the white candles. Then, one by one, he snuffs the candles. They can be pinched out or blown out; in this case it does not matter. What matters is that as each candle goes out, the entire groups says: "We thank You, and farewell." They then feel the Elementals leave.

Maintain silence for a short while—ten heartbeats is adequate. Then the person who cast the circle starts in the north and walks widdershins (counterclockwise) around the circle, saying:

> *Powers of Water, Wind, and Flame,*
> *Return to the Stone from which You came.*
> *The power we held we now release.*
> *The circle parts, but does not cease.*

Then all say in unison:

> *For merry did we meet,*
> *And merry shall we part,*
> *And merry meet again.*

Each person should now write down the message that was divined for him or her, and discuss it with the person who did the divination.

Part IV

Pitfalls and Possibilities

16

Words of Power, Sacred Languages, and Other Nonsense

ယာ

"But," I can hear you saying, "where are the magick words, the tones and syllables of power, the strange arcane names, the tongue mumbling gobbledygook?"

There aren't any.

The strange names and "words of power" are merely bad translations and bungled phonetic transliterations of ancient languages such as Semitic, Chaldean, and Egyptian. A thousand years ago, when literacy had almost been destroyed by the ruling theocratic church, a written word seemed magickal. That some marks on paper or parchment, or broken pot shards could hold and carry information, seemed wondrous. A foreign language that came complete with strange stories of an almost unbelievable culture and temporal power could impress the illiterate and the gullible. Look at what advertising can do today.

If you prefer to have words of power, make your own. If your feel enhanced and psychically strengthened by using an ancient language, study it. But before you sit down with *Sumerian for Beginners*, ask yourself this: "Can I really express myself better, or at least as well, in this old language than in my native tongue?" If you are honest, I think the answer will be no. In fact, doing so will probably slow you down, make you self- conscious, and inhibit your natural poetry. If you are a natural speaker of more than one language, choose the one that best echoes the rhythms and music of your soul.

17

Other Magickal Systems of Invocation and Evocation

ဢ

Invocation and evocation are not new. As I wrote in the opening chapter, people have been invoking and evoking Divinity ever since we came down from the trees, and who knows, we may have done it up there in the branches too. What is new is that most people think that to be able to do it you have to be either a very holy person—or a very wicked person.

The Greek-Egyptian Magical Papyri, a collection of magickal practices from about 300 C.E., has entire chapters on different types of invocations and evocations. Most of them have to do with summoning some lesser sort of God-form and directing Him (rarely a Her) to control, hex, kill, maim, or seduce someone else for the evoker. A close reading of the texts shows that by the time this anthology of manuscripts was put together, the priests in the temples were there to exercise secular power and not out of any spiritual or religious vocation.

Invocation and evocation played a very important role in the early Christian church, and in the New Testament we read how one church or another was speaking in tongues, summoning the "spirit of the Lord," and in general having a good time. But Paul, who reports these uses of "spiritual gifts," took a somewhat dim view of them, and subsequent bishops put an end to these magickal practices. By the late second century it was considered bad form, if not downright heresy, to claim to have invoked the spirit of Jesus Christ. The Gnostics, many of whom considered themselves good Christians, held on to these practices for several more centuries.

The idea of a God-form entering a human was also present in the early Judeo-Christian idea of demonic possession, a kind of "invocation" that was believed to be involuntary and, at least in some cases, permanent. The origins of this concept are obscure. One possible source is the labeling of the God-forms of competing religions as demons, so the priests and priestesses who invoked those God-forms were "possessed" by demons. Another source is mental illness, whether caused by organic illness (as may be the case in schizophrenia) or by some form of abuse. Victims of abuse, particularly child abuse, can form alternate personalities that are imitations of the abuser, and they can undergo episodes of "possession" when those personalities are in control.

In any case, the concept of demonic possession was present in Christianity from the beginning. Jesus and the apostles were believed to have practiced exorcism to drive out possessing demons, and the early followers of Jesus seem to have done so as well. As the other spiritual practices of the early Christians were gradually suppressed exorcism became less common, but unlike the literal invocation of the Holy Spirit, it was never entirely abandoned. By the Middle Ages, Christianity had developed and elaborated its mythology of the chief demon, the Devil, to the point where Christians saw the Devil's hand in all natural misfortune and human evil. The concept of demonic possession fit into this mythology perfectly. Some evildoers were tempted by the Devil, but the most shockingly wicked were directly possessed. The hold of this mythology on Western consciousness is hard to exaggerate. As late as the nineteenth and early twentieth centuries it was still common to refer to juvenile delinquents and especially vicious adult criminals as being possessed by the Devil. This history of cultural conditioning can explain why occasional cases of mental illness take the shape they do and are interpreted as they are.

In her book *Possession,* Erika Bourguignon, after examining hundreds of ethnological studies, found that the only people to suffer from possession by demons were Christians, and in a few cases, Jews. Other cultures which do not have a primary evil god-form simply do not have the psychological dysfunction that manifests itself as "possession by demons or the Devil."

Judeo-Christian demonology is the principal source for Enochian and Ceremonial magick. Many books have been written on these subjects, and a few novels as well.

John Dee, the man who claimed that he learned the Enochian alphabet and the accompanying magickal rituals from ancient Hebraic angels, was a genius. He spoke half a dozen languages fluently; in particular, he read and spoke Hebrew and Arabic, both of which languages had a magickal cachet in late-Renaissance Europe. He was a skilled mathematician and astrologer (everyone believed in astrology in the sixteenth century, even the pope). John Dee was also in fact, a spy for Queen Elizabeth I. He was so good that he may have been a quadruple agent, working for the papacy in Rome, the French, the Spanish, *and* the English.

It is very likely that the Enochian alphabet is a sophisticated espionage code. The trappings of Enochian magick were smoke and mirrors to hide the covert meetings and workings of his spy network. The magickal aura also attracted pretty women to him, and he made a nice secondary income from selling spells and 'hexes.' Regardless of the reality behind its beginnings, even today people believe in Enochian and ceremonial magick.

During the late nineteenth century, an upsurge of interest in things occult swept Europe. Perhaps this wave of pseudomagickal practice was given impetus by the archeological finds in Mideast and Egypt. Certainly, influences from India and Tibet fueled the interest of the reading public. The Parliament of Religions, held in Chicago in 1893, brought new and exciting ideas from the Orient to the West, and among them were old and almost totally misunderstood systems of magick.

In England, several very intelligent people took Enochian magick, and Masonic and Rosicrucian practices, blended them all with a goodly dollop of eastern mysticism, and created a magickal-religious group called the Golden Dawn. Waite, MacGregor Mathers, and Aleister Crowley are the most famous proponents of this belief system. A careful study of their lives with a modern perspective on their childhoods shows that every one of them had serious control issues. Each one, and Crowley in particular, had been seriously abused as a child—Crowley's own mother lamented that she had not beaten him enough! Both Mathers and Waite may have been sexually abused by their older schoolmates—but that was considered normal in the public (actually private) schools of wealthy ninteen-century England.

Israel Regardie's book *The Complete Golden Dawn System of Magic* goes into deep detail on how to evoke demons and other beings of power that will then somehow serve the purposes of the evoker. But careful reading of the book shows it to be an exercise in Judeo-Christian Gnosticism. And indeed, within that belief system demons can most certainly be evoked, but the demons will come from the evoker's internal nightmares, not from any place of power or supernatural energy.

18

Modern Magicians, Fakes, and Frauds

ഗ

Although there are many sincere people who have real invocative and evocative experiences, there are many who do not and yet claim they do, usually for personal power and gain. It is best to enter into any study with a certain skepticism. Don't believe anything until you are satisfied that it works for you.

In the mid 1970s, I had two very enlightening experiences which taught me a lot about what worked for me, and also about how dangerous the twisted workings of monotheistic belief systems can be. The first was a three-month jaunt into the territory of ceremonial magick. I had read some books on ceremonial magick and was curious as to whether or not these practices, based on medieval Jewish Kabbalah, were effective: Did they result in real manifestations, or were the "results" simply the products of superstitious minds and damaged spirits?

Remember, this was the mid 1970s; the New Age movement was just a distant glimmer in some merchandiser's eye. There were almost no occult bookstores, and any magickal group was likely to be very secretive. There really wasn't any way to "comparison shop." After much searching I met a man who claimed that he was a powerful magickian, and he certainly seemed—at least to the gullible person I was at the time—to have some arcane and occult abilities.

I will call him John Doe. Tall, blond, with piercing blue eyes and a boyish smile, he was charismatic and dynamic, witty and polished. John possessed a fascinating intelligence that floated on a deeper and dangerously seductive darkness. Young people flocked about him like pigeons around a person with bread-crumbs in the park.

His method of entrapping young people was subtle and effective. He hinted that he was able to teach techniques of incredible power, but he seemed very loath to share them. He made you really struggle and strive to get invited to one of his evocative rituals—as he called his late-night meetings. He also charged large amounts of money for his classes, for he knew what every wise man knows, that once a person has paid hard cash for anything they will defend the effectiveness and rightness of whatever they bought even in the face of the most clear and damning contrary evidence.

I didn't have any money to pay for his classes but I was tenacious, and I was finally "allowed" to attend a working that he performed in his apartment in central Chicago.

It was a large and beautifully decorated apartment—something out of *Architectural Digest*—and except for the odd statue here and there, and what I believe was a real Klimt painting, no one who had casually entered the apartment would have guessed that this was the home of a great and potent magickian.

There were about twenty people there that night, only a few of whom I knew. Several of the older people (remember, I was in my mid-twenties, so anyone in their forties was ancient) sat apart from the rest and seemed to be in their own world, only deigning to notice the rest of us when they wanted something from the kitchen. The "newbies" fetched and carried gladly for the seasoned retainers of the "great man."

The night grew late and the candles started to gutter out, and the promised manifestation of elemental demons seemed no more imminent than it had at noon. Finally we were ushered into a room that was decorated with a strange mix of Kabbalistic diagrams, vampire symbolism, Egyptian temple art, and Manhattan grossness. A huge red circle was painted on the floor; inside that was a black square, and inside that was a white triangle. Strange numerical sigils inscribed on what looked like clay tablets were scattered about. He may actually have known something about Sumerian cuneiform, but I doubt the sigils were in anything except modern hen-scratch.

The man entered, dressed in a stunning gold lamé robe; a conical hat, similar to the pope's tiara, wobbled on his head. He washed his hands in a silver bowl, muttering spells in some arcane language—at the time I assumed it was Hebrew, but now I think it was garbled nonsense meant to impress the masses.

He lit incense, and a tiny nervous woman in a hideous black and red robe hurried about the room lighting a dozen or so candles. The rest of us stood where we were put, and were warned repeatedly to remain within the "precinct of power" for our own protection.

Then he proceeded to summon forth demons. He started to chant in his arcane language. The chanting became droning. This went on for many long minutes.

More incense was thrown on the charcoal and the droning became growling and the growling became ranting. Except for the heavy breathing of the young woman next to me, our leader was the only one making any noise. The angelic sounds that we were supposed to hear came from a poorly concealed tape recorder tucked behind a nicely drawn image of the Winged Sephiroth.

Gullible I may have been, but I saw and heard nothing magickal. More important, I felt nothing except the twisted energy of a number of eager, overwrought people. What I did see was a man working himself into hysteria, and as he did so, several of the people around me also became hysterical. They began to babble incoherently, and one began to chew on her arm until she broke the skin and drew blood. Two of the hysterical people began to get physically abusive to one another, while others started having fits. The situation moved from unpleasant to ugly, and I broke the so-called circle of protection and left.

I ran. Nothing happened to me; no howling demons pursued me; no rash of bad luck plagued my life. In fact, things got better, probably because I wasn't wasting energy on John Doe anymore.

For some time after that I received threatening phone calls and letters from him and his adherents, but nothing came of the threats. I moved, they lost interest, and the whole thing resolved into an unpleasant taste in my mouth.

Later I learned, from the nervous woman in the ugly black and red robe, that the man had not only been severely abused by a minister in his youth, but was, at the time the "ceremony" took place, actively abusing both his children from his two previous marriages. And later I learned that he was, at least at that time, a heavy drug user and had been supplying several of the members of his group with drugs. The nervous woman was deeply infatuated with the man, and even as she told me the sordid details of his life she could see nothing wrong in what he was doing. She took his abuse as proof that he was powerful and his drug use as evidence that he was a free soul.

If he summoned demons, they were his own, and the only thing they did was allow him to displace his own sense of helplessness, his repressed pain, and his very justified and righteous anger at the vicious abuse he had suffered onto others. Yet, whatever had happened to him as a child did not excuse his actions as an adult. His behavior was totally unethical and illegal. He had neither magick nor power, and in retrospect I am fairly confident that if he ever did have a genuine invocation of Divinity he quickly repressed the memory of it and went on to more profitable practices.

Soon after that incident he stopped being a ceremonial

magickian and became in turn an American aboriginal shaman, a Sufi mystic, a born-again Christian preacher, and a Buddhist monk. The last I heard he had come full circle and was, once more, an ascended Gnostic master. But no matter what substance he uses or what belief system he buys into, the demons he evokes are his own ugly and repressed memories. It is regrettable that such a person is able to entrap others to help him play out his fantasies.

The second incident occurred in the fall of 1977, when I had a chance to go to New York City. While there, I was introduced to a man who owned one of the few publicly known occult bookstores. I don't know why he took a liking to me, as I found out later that liking people was not his usual wont, but perhaps he was trying to impress the young man who was traveling with me.

In any event, after a long evening of discussion he told my companion and me that the most famous book ever written on the subject of demonology was in fact a joke that he and a friend of his, a well-known horror writer, had put together as a hoax. Indeed, if you happen upon the book and read the introduction with that information in mind you will see that the authors are telling you exactly that: The book is a hoax and has no sources of ancient manuscript, papyri, or clay tablets. It was conceived of and written during the middle of the twentieth century. The authors did not intend the book to be taken seriously, and the gentleman with whom I visited was vastly amused that so many people did, and still do.

The *Necronomicon* has no basis in fact. It is a work of fiction. But it has power, yes, that it does. I know more than one young person who found themselves thoroughly scared out of their wits by that book, and considering the skill with which it was crafted and the literary genius behind it, that is not surprising. What I find amazing and alarming is that many people—obviously badly abused and desperately seeking to possess power over others— use this book as a basis for their magickal and spiritual practices.

It has the power to evoke all the twistings and turnings of a tortured soul who has survived by forgetting what happened. It has the power to make otherwise sane people do idiotic things, and the power to engage with those same people's need to suffer and inflict suffering on others. But the book has no supernatural or divine power.

Having observed with my own eyes the effects of so-called Enochian or ceremonial magicks, and having discovered a rare truth about an influential book, I began to do some debunking studies.

For a long time I was convinced that any kind of evocative ritual was based on hoax, greed, and personal subliminal emotional agendas. And in point of fact, any ritual whose message is to injure or harm, whose effects are to belittle or disempower people, most likely is. I am still extremely skeptical of mystical messages, especially when they include exhortations to send money, transcend the flesh, or practice vegetarianism.

Divine Apprehension Gone Awry: Three Case Studies

There have been, and most likely will continue to be, people who become convinced that not only has an aspect of the Divine emanated through them, communicating with them and through them to other people, but that they are in fact the One God, incarnated. When this happens, the person is most likely to make his experience fit into the belief system that he has internalized from his culture.

One of the most famous of all these people was a man named Meher Baba, who claimed to be the avatar of Divinity. Meher Baba (Merwan Sheriar Irani) was born in Poona, India, in 1894. Although his parents were ethnically Persian, he was educated at a Roman Catholic high school in Poona, and at the age of nineteen he had an intense religious and spiritual experience. It was probably a sexual initiation, but many years later he wrote a more acceptable account: that he had been struck in the head with a rock flung by a holy yogi.

For the next nine years he studied both Sufi and Hindu spiritual practices, and he "realized" that he was not a human at all, but the avatar of God, a being who had graciously taken on human form to communicate and teach others.

A diligent study of Baba's sayings (actually his writings, since he decided that avatars shouldn't talk), which were further transcribed and expanded by his students, show that while he was a gentle and enlightened person for his culture and time, his philosophies were rehashings and blendings of Sufism and Hindu Atmanism. They are life-denying, ascetic, monastic, and intolerant of the physical body, sexual needs and desires, and especially femaleness. According to Meher Baba, all these things stand between a human being and transcendence.

Meher Baba declared that one must decide that either he was a fraud or what he said he was, God. (The same argument has been used by C. S. Lewis on behalf of Jesus' divinity.) He never allowed for the middle ground—he might be simply a human being doing something that humans beings are able to do: experience God directly. Meher Baba died in 1969.

There is presently a woman in India who goes by the title of the Mother. She also claims to be God, no mere Avatar-hood about it. She has declared that the possession a human flesh-and-blood body is a spiritual hindrance. Notice, however, that even in her belief system God needs a body to teach and communicate.

Her writings fill volumes. Those I have read manifest a real hatred of humanity and all that being human entails. On the surface she is sweetness and light, but the underlying message is quite clear: if you want to be holy, if you want to be in direct communication with Divinity, you must practice all sorts of life-denying ascetic austerities—and especially, send her money. Life may be worthless, but money is fine.

Another example of a spontaneous invocation and Divine manifestation that probably did occur and yet may have gone awry is the case of Franz Bardon. In Czechoslovakia during the

early part of the twentieth century, a young man named Franz
Bardon had what seems to be a spontaneous invocation of
Divinity.

Bardon was raised in the brutal Roman Catholic society that
permeated eastern Europe in the early twentieth century. What
little is known of his childhood indicates he was, at the very
least, severely physically abused and probably emotionally and
psychically abused as well. Franz somehow remained an
intelligent and sensitive child who was still open to ecstatic
manifestation into his adolescent years.

He was about fourteen at the time of the first experience, and
the God-form was, as he later reported, consistent with his
Christian background. He had several such manifestations and
he found, between his Christianity and Gnosticism, a way of
explaining what happened to him. It appears that he did not stay
Christian for very long. Soon he was heavily involved in
ceremonial magick and Enochian sorcery.

Whatever happened to young Franz was certainly powerful.
It may have been an adolescent sexual encounter that he later
transformed into an ecstatic manifestation—some of his writings suggest this—or it may have been a spontaneous invocation.
Whatever it was, it helped him to survive three-and-a-half years
in a Nazi concentration camp. When he emerged from the camp
with the other survivors, he became increasingly convinced that
not only had he been visited by a god, but he was the living
incarnation of his god. At some point he became convinced that
he had never been human, that he had always been God.

His teachings have followed the same life-denying ascetic
pattern that characterizes most pseudo-Christian and neo-
Gnostic belief systems. Various types of discipline—fasting, sleep
and sensory deprivation, vegetarian diets, sexual abstinence, or
sex performed to increase psychic powers—fill the first volume
of his writings.

His second book of writings is full of neo-Gnostic foolishness:
genies, demons, elemental intelligences, spheres of planetary

influences, and other nonsense for chapter after chapter. He tells you how to use rituals of purification to free talismans of base earthly connections, how to summon spirits of immense power to do your bidding, and how to impress people and gain influence over them.

Franz Bardon died in 1958 in a Czech prison—incarcerated for possessing illegal substances. His followers have always insisted that he was imprisoned on false charges because the Communist government was afraid of his powers.

I mention Franz Bardon for a specific purpose: although few people have heard of him or read his books, he is a good example in support of my contention that Ceremonial (Enochian) magick does not work. If it did work, the many practitioners of those sorceries and ceremonial invocative and evocative rituals would enjoy the fruits of their labors, and they don't. If one could summon genies to see through walls, bring treasure, smite one's enemies, or seduce one's reluctant lover, then one would have these things occur. They didn't occur for Franz Bardon.

His methods of making a talisman under the planetary spheres of Jupiter and Mercury, using the intelligence of Ish-Raph-El, will supposedly endow the possessor with the ability to unlock doors. Other charms and spells in his books tell you how to assure victory in legal situations. Still others promise wealth.

But the doors remained locked on Franz. His pockets were always empty and the forces of his society moved against him at every turn. With all of his magickal "power," Bardon had none of its benefits. He also seems to have been an almost destitute alcoholic who may have had black-market connections. It is impossible to tell, given the corrupt system that was in power in Czechoslovakia at the time. His story is tragic, not only because of the pain and suffering that he endured, but because he was obviously an intelligent and sensitive man. I wonder what he could have achieved if he had not wasted his time on ceremonial magick and Enochian angels.

People who are drawn to ceremonial magick and Enochian

magicks are people who at some deep level are feeling hopeless and powerless, and desperately need to have some "other" come and kick their oppressors in the butt. It doesn't work that way. Ceremonial magick does not work because Divinity doesn't use the methods of "summon," "command," "constrain," or "force."

Meher Baba, Franz Bardon, and the Mother are good examples of Divinity's willingness to reach out and communicate with anyone who will allow communication.

Unfortunately, far too often those to whom Divinity has manifested Itself become entrapped by the cultures that surround them.

Culture says that access to Divinity requires self-denial and control over oneself: sexual abstinence, bodily deprivation, myriad forms of denial, and physically punitive practices. So all three of our examples have used and advocated various forms of such practices.

Culture says contact with Divinity is the result of personal merit, and since it is so rare, anyone who has it must be extremely meritorious and special. When a person believes something like this about himself or herself, the gratification it brings can be addictive. Perhaps this is why all three of our examples came to the point of claiming to be God Himself or Herself.

Culture says that contact with Divinity should bring with it the respect, adulation, and obedience of others. So Meher Baba and the Mother expected such responses, and for the most part received them. Franz Bardon, who did not receive them very much, may have been trying to use ceremonial magick as a substitute.

I know I have written the same things earlier, but I feel the point cannot be made too strongly. Our world culture, north and south, east and west, has a very odd concept of what Divinity wants and what it takes to be "holy" or "good enough" to be in communication with Divinity. When Divinity says, "All I want from you is your laughter..." our culturally disciplined expectations are hard pressed to believe it. I am confident that when you have experienced Divinity you *will* believe it.

Divinity will never ask that you mutilate your children, much less sacrifice them, or return their spiritual essence to the All-father. Divinity will never ask you to starve your body or keep your mind in ignorance.

Divinity will not require you to wear special clothing, cover your face, perform special types of physical exercises, or wear special jewelry. Divinity doesn't care about any of those human customs.

Divinity doesn't care what you eat as long as what you eat keeps you healthy, and Divinity doesn't care what you drink as long as that drink does not abuse you or others.

Divinity will not tell you with whom to have sex, or when, or to have limited and specific purposes in mind when you have sex. All those beliefs have been imposed on humanity by humans who have used them to exert control.

Divinity has never ordered a war, massacre, pogrom, or jihad. Divinity doesn't express Itself in bullets and bombs. Again, those are human ways of handling strife.

Divinity expresses Itself as often through the female form as through the male, and has never decreed that the male form is superior. That is a human concept used to keep half the human race in subjection.

Divinity has no preference for skin color, eye color, or texture of hair. Divinity is as available to people in the West as in the East, and in the southern hemisphere as in the northern. Divinity can be found on a lonely mountain and in a city ghetto. There is no specific sacred city or place. All are sacred, as are all human beings.

19

Drugs, Alcohol, and Physical Deprivation as Aids to Invocation and Evocation

༩ⓒ

For thousands of years, if we believe historians and anthropologists, shamans and other religious people have used drugs, alcohol, and bodily deprivation to enhance, and in some cases, to enable communication with Divinity. Siberian shamans used poisonous mushrooms, which in controlled doses send the user into ecstatic trance. Yaqui shamans use datura, peyote, and other cacti, and the poisons made from frogs to do the same. In the mid 1960s, Timothy Leary conducted experiments with LSD and found that he and his fellows had intense spiritual experiences.

In ancient Greece, the followers of Dionysus used wine, probably heavily laced with opium, to achieve religious frenzy, and some scholars believe that the ingestion of sacred mushrooms was part of the early Christian cults' rituals.

Hashish in the Middle East, drugged honey wine in Europe—wherever you look, drugs have a long historical connection with religious practices and especially with the rituals of invocation and evocation.

I strongly suggest that you stay far away from them. Not because they will do you hideous damage—although there is always that possibility. I make this recommendation primarily because they are usually illegal, and because they are illegal the acts of obtaining them and using them have serious consequences in the secular world. Also, they aren't really that effective. They represent a big risk in return for a minor enhancement of genuine religious experience.

Drugs can have an intense psychological and emotional effect. They can "show" you aspects of reality that you had no idea existed; they can take you "places." Drugs can open you up, and in the proper hands, I assume that they can allow you to step outside of the imposed boundaries of our religiously barren landscape. But I have never found that they made the experience of Divine Invocation more effective or more "real." In fact, the use of alcohol and hallucinogenic drugs usually interferes with the experience because afterwards you are never sure what was caused by Divinity and what resulted from the drug.

I must be honest here and admit that I speak from report rather than from experience. I have never used drugs to enhance or enable my invocation or evocations. I have never had the need. However, I have been told by several people that no matter how effective they seem at the time, hours or days after using drugs to achieve invocation or evocation doubts begin to set in, then questions and fears, and in a while the entire experience wears the "Was it real?" label. Perhaps the best way to explain this is to recount the story that a young man for whom I have deep respect told me.

I'll call him George. He had worked with my coven for some years and then had the opportunity to move to California and continue his education. While there, George and a group of friends from the university met what seemed to have been a genuine Yaqui shaman who lived in western Mexico. The shaman was visiting the university and gave a series of lectures in the folklore department. After one lecture George and his friends went out for drinks with the Mexican gentleman. A long-term friendship was forged that resulted in George going to Mexico and studying for some months with the shaman. While there, George had several wondrous and exciting experiences.

One morning at about 4:00 A.M. I received a call from him. He was in California on the beach at Monterey, calling from a cellular phone. Obviously in a state of expanded consciousness and extreme excitement, he proceeded to talk to me as though I were in the room with him. He had had a powerful apprehension of Divinity earlier in the day and was still feeling connected to all of creation. He told me that everything had a different deeper and more significant color, colors seemed to have taste and taste evoked musical tones. He had seen himself and me in a garden, where we had become plants and the plants had become people. He went on and on and I soon ceased to write down what he was saying, preferring to listen. After about three hours he drifted off and I hung up. But I could not sleep. Something was bothering me, something George hadn't told me.

What I had figured out was that he and his friends had decided to duplicate one of the spiritual rituals that he had studied with the Yaqui shaman. They had obtained some hallucinogenic mushrooms, fasted, and taken the mushrooms after soaking them in mezcal. Later I learned that the experiences lasted all night and into the next day.

But there George and his friends got into trouble. They had all taken the mushrooms, and therefore no one was competent to take care of them. Some of the young people became dehydrated; others started to vomit continuously. For some, the ecstatic experience changed into nightmares. By the end of the day, two of the group were in the hospital and George was very sick.

After this happened I didn't hear from him for several months, except a short call to tell me he was feeling better and that he had decided not to return to Mexico that fall. In fact, he came back to Philadelphia on his way to transferring to a graduate program in the Midwest.

We spent a couple of afternoons together and he told that me that, as much as he had learned from the shaman, he felt he would always regret the unsupervised ritual using the mushrooms. I asked him why. He gazed into space for a while and then said, with a wry smile, "What I encountered was pure bliss. I felt that I was in the presence of a form of Divinity that was almost exactly what you have described on many occasions. What Divinity told me was so life-affirming, so absolutely accepting of me and all of my experiences, it seemed that I was completely connected with the entirety of creation. And yet I will never be sure; I can never know for certain if it was truly Divinity or wishful thinking and mushrooms."

George had learned much, but the use of the hallucinogenic substance had deprived him of the subjective certainty that comes from invocation and evocation, and that is so central to the resulting personal growth and transformation.

Don't do that to yourself, or to your spiritual rituals.

Abuse of alcohol results in similar stories, except that alcohol is a poison which, in small quantities, helps us relax and depresses the central nervous system, removing inhibitions. In small amounts, alcohol may be conducive to effective invocation. In *small* amounts. A four-ounce glass of wine before ritual will not interfere, and if you are particularly stressed it may help. But if you have to get drunk to achieve invocation or evocation, you aren't really achieving anything but liver and brain damage.

Food can be a good transitional medium from ordinary space into sacred space, but only if it is prepared and eaten with intention. Ordering in a pizza and wolfing it down is not what I mean.

A carefully prepared loaf of bread, made from scratch, kneaded and baked with careful attention to the process of creation and transmutation and then eaten with intent can be a powerful tool when invoking a Grain Goddess. The same is true of preparing and eating a piece of meat when invoking a god of the hunt. But too much food before a ritual can slow you down, make you drowsy, and prevent you from being fully present during the ritual.

Physical deprivation is another traditional way of preparing the mind for invocation or evocation. These practices, usually ascetic in nature, have many different effects on the body and not all are positive. Throughout the world, ascetic practices have a very long history. Unfortunately, they remain popular in the present day. Perhaps the most depressing experience I had in writing this book was my research into modern mystical groups. Several thousand groups are represented on the World Wide Web, and *all* of those that I glanced at and the four hundred I read about at some length are focused on life-denial. They try to approach Divinity through control of the body, methods of purification, transcending physical limitations, rising above physical attachments, and other similar means.

The idea of denying life and the body pervades all of these groups regardless of their underlying belief systems. From Tibetan Bon to Judaic Kabbalah, Islamic Suni and Sufi practices to New Age angelics, the theme is constant: leave the body, get off the earth, surrender, and be saved. It does not matter what the actual mechanism of salvation is supposed to be—cognitive knowing, or redemption purchased by some sacrifice on the part of a Divinity. In each case the individual can achieve it only by practices that treat the body and the senses as obstacles to be enlightened, transcended, overcome, mastered, or conquered.

Some common characteristics of these groups should serve as warnings. First, controlling the body, its needs and desires, is treated as more important than actually achieving communication with Divinity. Second, the emphasis is on rising above the pain of life or surrendering to the will of Divinity rather than the more difficult and socially dangerous process of healing. Third, these groups judge the aspirant's progress by his or her unquestioning obedience to the group's teacher or master. (This last is not only damaging but dangerous. From such modes of thinking come incidents such as the insanity of the Branch Davidians in Waco, Texas, Islamic mandates for murder such as the one currently out against Salmon Rushdie, and other religious persecutions.)

I am adamantly against any kind of fasting, purging, or other food deprivations. Depriving the body and throwing it into chemical imbalance is a dangerous way of trying to achieve an altered state of consciousness. Most forms of physical deprivation do not increase the capacity to communicate directly with Divinity; instead, they take emotional and psychic resources and squander them on social-control issues.

20

Sex as an Aid to Invocation and Evocation

ΩΩΩ

While almost all mystical belief systems either flatly deny the use of sexuality and sexual practice as a means of enhancing or enabling invocation, or—as is most common—consider sexual desire a contemptible and degrading animal appetite, some belief systems, such as Tantric Yoga, do acknowledge the inherent power that lies within human sexuality.

Sexuality and sexual practices are among the oldest and most powerful aids to invocation and evocation. They are on a par with drumming and chanting for trance induction, Divine manifestation, and personal apprehension of Divinity; but unlike drumming and chanting, sexuality and sexual practices are among the most difficult aids to invocation and evocation to use effectively.

I state this not as either judgment or comment on sex, but as a sad truth about the miserable state of affairs in which our pan-world culture finds itself with regards to sexuality and sexual practices. I have yet to meet a person over the age of five who hasn't had their sexuality damaged by our culture, and it doesn't matter on what continent they were born or whether they live in a rural or urban area. Asia and Europe, South America and Africa, Australia and North America—the damage is everywhere.

In the early 1980s, while attending West Chester University, I worked with some other students on a research project run by one of our sociology professors. I had the happy task of reading a great deal of modern pornography and charting themes within the stories, although I was spared the Victorian pornography with its omnipresent theme of child molestation.

The graphic sexual encounters did not bother me. What I found disturbing was the preponderance of sado-masochism and fantasies of rape, abduction, sex-with-a-passing-stranger, physical abuse, emotional abuse, and more. Even in the pages of romantic novels, sexuality often has a theme of unwilling ravishment that turns into passionate love.

This is the cultural air we breathe. It teaches us that autoeroticism is dirty and shameful, but it equates other sexual relationships with the power to manipulate others: power to obtain favors, physical goods, social status, and career mentoring, ad nauseam. This means that if you try to use your innate sexual powers to help you achieve invocation or evocation, you will most likely encounter serious problems. If you intend to use sex and the various sexual practices that are effective for inducing and enabling invocation and evocation, you need to rid yourself of the twist that sexuality has been given by all the religions of the world.

The cleansing and healing meditations that are given in the first section of the book need to be repeated, but with clear focus on your sexuality, sexual practices, and sexual needs. Be prepared to encounter a great deal of resistance from your inner self, ranging anywhere from internal comments that "this is bad" or "this is nasty" to anhedonic repression of sexual feelings and physical numbness in the genitals. In addition, you will experience a great deal of opposition from almost anyone with whom you attempt to use sexual energies to achieve or enhance invocation or evocation.

Having written that in the spirit of "Don't say I didn't warn you," let me now focus on the positive aspects.

Sex is powerful. The emotional and physical feelings that are aroused by sex greatly enhance divine apprehension and make both invocation and evocation easier. People in a state of extreme sexual arousal almost invoke spontaneously, and reports from around the world describing the sensations and emotional feelings during climax indicate that at that moment and for some time afterward, ecstatic spiritual feelings and inspiration often occur. I believe that it is this fact which inspired Gerald Gardner to create the lovely ritual called "Drawing Down the Moon." However, I have never seen that ritual actually achieve manifestation of Deity—although not for want of trying on the part of the participants.

In my opinion there are two likely reasons for this. First, it is probably impossible for someone to use their power to make a space in another person in which Divinity would manifest itself. The danger of the abuse of power in such a situation is far too great, and Divinity will not abuse the person who is the "container." If invocation does occur, it is because the person into whom the aspect of Divinity is being drawn actually invokes for herself or himself. Second, everyone I know has some remnant of Judeo-Christianity in their background and is unable to overcome those life-hating tendencies in the presence of an audience.

Sexual practices to aid and enhance both invocation and evocation are probably best done in privacy. No one needs the extra burden of having to perform in front of an audience as well as having to perform sexually.

Autoeroticism is the best, and for most of us the only place to start. Learning to love oneself and give pleasure to oneself without going into abusive fantasies—of whatever flavor—is the first step in learning to use sexuality to enable and enhance the rituals of invocation and evocation.

To work with your own psychic talents to learn to manipulate the energy of pleasure so that Divinity can manifest itself is not an easy task, nor one that you will learn rapidly. Once you have learned how to achieve climax without using abuse fantasies or "power-over" fantasies (the ones where you use, abuse, trick, hurt, molest, manipulate, or coerce another), you are ready to use that energy to invoke.

The next section presents a rough outline for such a ritual.

The Sacred Rite of Venery

Secure your room. Make sure the phone is disconnected and the door is locked. Take special care in cleaning and decorating the room. Flowers, a light incense, a glass of wine or sparkling water, perhaps a piece of chocolate or (if you prefer) another small sweet.

Take a bath and rub yourself all over with a light oil. Comb your hair, brush your teeth, make yourself feel pretty. (Gentlemen: You are hereby given permission to be "pretty." Goddess likes "pretty" men. She told me so.)

Put on some soothing romantic music, turn down the lights, and begin to masturbate, using whatever technique you have found most effective for you. As your sensual pleasure rises, pretend you are making love to a God (actually, you are). Make the fantasy as real and vivid as you are able.

Speak out loud, allow your "pretender"—that powerful magickal tool I wrote about earlier—to speak for the God or Goddess. When you achieve climax, "share" the pleasure with the God-form. My experience and the experience of others who have used this very simple and yet very effective technique is that the pleasure seems to double and last much longer than normal.

When you are able to consistently achieve this kind of invocation with masturbation, try it with a willing partner. Decide ahead of time on a purpose for the ritual. In the beginning, choose god-forms with whom you are familiar and intimate. As with the solitary ritual, have the space secure and beautiful. Take hours, instead of minutes, to get ready. Do the simplest things for each other, feed each other, hold each other's glass while drinking, help each other bathe. Wear beautiful and sensual lingerie, carefully apply makeup to each other. (Again, gentlemen: Gods like men in mascara. So do Goddesses. And men in skirts are Divine.)

Anoint each other with lightly scented oil, naming each other by the name of the previously agreed-upon God-form. Begin the love-making, always keeping in mind that you are making love to Divinity. As the sexual pleasure increases, give in to it. Do not try to control it; just let it happen. When it does happen, you will experience something totally unique. I will not even begin to try to relate some of the experiences that I and others have had. This space needs to be totally your own without any preconception.

If at any point in the ritual you find yourself having doubts, fears, or slipping into abusive fantasies, stop the ritual and talk it over with your partner. Try to find out what triggered you in the situation. Change that triggering factor and try again. If you find you are being triggered more than once, stop that ritual and go back to the solitary practice until you have unkinked whatever it was that was blocking you in the partnered ritual.

I have been asked if the Ritual of Venery is limited to two people. I see no inherent reason why that should be so, as long as everyone involved is utterly clear and agrees on the purpose, is free of and healed of abuse and abusive sexual issues and totally respecting of everyone else, has all their needs met, *and* can overcome the terrific negative onus that our society places on group sex. This is a tall order, but I am certain that somewhere there are some brave and shining souls who have achieved it.

21

Finding the Web of All-Being

ᏯᏨ

As you work with the meditations and rituals in this book, as you heal and grow, there will come a time when you will experience what, in my opinion, is the most powerful spiritual and religious experience possible. At some point, when you are in direct one-on-one communication with Divinity, you will find yourself in the middle of an immense infinitely stranded web of Energy.

At every point where the strands meet, cross, knot together, split, and reweave themselves, an intelligent sentient being exists. This may be a human from the third planet of the star Sol. It may be an intelligent being from a different and far distant solar system, but you will find that you can communicate clearly with any and all of these beings.

Some will know you, as though they have met you but you failed to notice them at the time. Others will greet you for the first time, and some you will suddenly recognize, realizing that you have indeed interacted with them on previous occasions.

None of these beings are your spiritual superiors, none are so-called ascended masters. Some may know more than you about certain subjects, but then you will know more about other matters than they. Everyone is on their own unique growth path and no one is better or more advanced than another. We are all here to grow, and we are all here to help each other.

The Web of All-being includes everything you can imagine and everything you can't. It is the matrix of all thingness and the crucible of the no-particular-thingness of probability. The energy of all thought, emotions, and experiences flows along the strands of the web, into the glowing core that pulses in the center. Everything you do, think, and feel contributes to the energy of the Web. No one is more important than anyone else in the Web. No one is evil or morally wrong simply because they made mistakes from which they are still learning (translation: still paying for those mistakes karmically).

As the energy flows through the strands into the core, another kind of energy flows out of the core and through the strands, invigorating and caressing each being at each node. As you become familiar with the Web of All-being, you will realize that the brain and nerves of our own physical body are a sort of crude approximation.

Here is the analogy: imagine that all sentient beings—and that can include trees, animals, and creatures that have no physical manifestation that we can detect—are the nerve endings of an incredibly complex nervous system. These "nerve endings"—sensory receptors—come into contact with stim-uli—some challenge, present problems, create puzzles. The receptors react to the stimuli. A message goes through the connecting strands of the web—the axons—and into the central core where the information is processed, analyzed, compared, stored, and a reaction impulse is sent back along the strands to the sensory receptor—the sentient being—who then uses the transformed information to experience the stimuli again but in a different and changed manner.

To continue to use this grossly simplified model, sentient beings such as human are the learning apparatus for the Divinity which is the Universe. And the more we experience and learn, the more energy Divinity has to give us.

She once told me that we humans were her energy dynamos, that we make more than we consume. The more we learn, the more healed and functional we become, the more energy there is in the Universe for us to continue to learn, grow, and experience the never-ending infinite wonders that Divinity Is. And so someday, when you are dancing on the Web of All-being, you and I shall meet. And it is my dearest wish that when we do, we will say, "Well Met and Merry Met, And Merry Meet Again."

SUGGESTED READING

Although I have been careful not to fill this book with footnotes and citations, listing specific books only when necessary, I do suggest that you at least take a look at some of the books from which my material was drawn. Unfortunately, you cannot read my journal or Book of Shadows, but you can create your own.

Background books are important, as is an open mind. Some of these books are vicious life-hating manifestos of authoritarian control; others are well meaning and genuine. Read them, consider them, but don't believe them!

Read with care, approach with caution, and always ask yourself: What do they want from me? Obedience? Money? Power over my life? Blind acceptance of dictates of behavior? Always decide for yourself if the actions and beliefs will make your mundane life and your spiritual one deeper, more fulfilling, and more functional—or less so.

Baba, Meher. *God Speaks*. (Sufism Reoriented LTD.: 1997)
Bardon, Franz. *Practice of Magical Evocation*. Marcher, 1991.
Bible (New Jerusalem Edition)
Brumby, Robert. *Dr. John Dee—the Original 007*. (out of print)
Clubb, Sir John. *The Lives and Times of Muhammad*. Chelsea, Michigan: Scarborough House, 1970.
Fox, Robin Lane. *Pagans and Christians*. New York: Harper, 1986.
————. *The Unauthorized Version*. New York: Vintage, 1993.
Fried, Jennifer J., *Betrayal Trauma*. Cambridge, Mass.: Harvard Univ. Press, 1996.

Jonas, Hans. *The Gnostic Religion.* Boston: Beacon Press, 1958.

The Koran (Try to get a recent translation.)

Kramer, Joel, and Elsted, Diane, et al. *The Guru Papers: Masks of Authoritarian Power.* Berkeley, Calif.: North Atlantic Books, 1993.

Miller, Alice. *Banished Knowledge.* New York: Doubleday, 1991.

_____. *Breaking Down the Wall of Silence.* New York: Meridian, 1993.

_____. *For Your Own Good.* New York: Doubleday, 1990.

_____. *Thou Shalt Not Be Aware.* New York: Doubleday, 1991.

The Rig Veda (almost impossible to get a complete edition, but *A Sourcebook in Indian Philosophy,* by Sarvepalli Radhakrishnan and Charles Moore, Princeton, 1957 is a good place to start)

Sherman, William H., *John Dee, the Politics of Reading and Writing in the English Renaissance.* Univ. of Mass., 1997.

Store, Anthony. *Feet of Clay.* San Diego: The Free Press, 1997.

King, Francis, and Skinner, Stephen. *Techniques of High Magick.* Inner Traditions, 1991.

There are, of course, many other worthwhile sources, as well as thousands of sites on the Internet.